It's On Repeat

It's
On
Repeat

a novel

by

Lance Nation

[signature]

many of the stories I shared with Jeff gave a few of these stories a bit of detail... especially NYC!

It's On Repeat is a work of fiction. Names, places, characters, and incidents are the products of the author's imagination or are used fictitiously. Any resemblance to actual persons, living or dead, events, or locales is entirely coincidental.

Copyright © Lance Edwin Nation Jr. 2021

Dedicated to the women in my life. You have led me where I am today.

To those I have hurt, I am deeply *sorry*. It was from my own pain I caused yours. —LN

Special thanks to The Queen of Tanna, PDTen, Chinese Food Buffets, Probably K, & Lumi. You were gusty enough to read this when it was still a conception, well before it was edited, finished, or printed. Thank you for your encouragement and criticisms. I needed to be humbled.

Finally, while editing this book, one of my closest friends died. His life was beautiful yet, like so many of us, he was haunted. A portion from each sale of this novel will go to help those struggling with addiction, overcome their demons, and find hope for today.

It's On Repeat

Now

Colin

Beneath the stone pedestal, at the feet of Ireland's Great Emancipator, Colin sits and sips his bottom shelf whiskey from a dented tin flask. The cold night sobers his mind and the booze warms his body. He could avoid most of the wind one street off the river but the salty taste and industrial smell from the brackish water is one of the last loves he has in Ireland. A lightly salted beard of two weeks protects his face and dark hair twists out from beneath a navy cap that covers his ears. His dark eyes are set in lighter circles and the weakened tissues under his eyes date him. A brown wool jacket, stained and worn, and loose jeans hide his hollow frame. Walking the same streets for some time now his feet had taken him here, to the O'Connell Monument, from memories: west on George Quay, over the River Liffey to avoid the Dark Horse Inn, left on Eden Quay, right on Marlborough St, and left down the first alley to avoid the Laughter Lounge and to circle back to Eden Quay. He avoids those bars, tired of the price of drinks, and even more so the conversations. Instead he wanders the streets drinking the whiskey he traded his gloves for. He takes another sip then pockets the flask. Stiff from the cold metal, the joints grate and scrape together as he opens and closes his hand.

Osteoarthritis,
Boats tied to a pier during a storm,
The boats, the bones, they grind each away with nothing in between to stop them

Beside him, sit two angels atop two teeth of the stone drum at the plinth of the pedestal. Cast in bronze, the winged victories, Patriotism and Fidelity, are guardians. Patriotism, armed with a sword and shield, and Fidelity guarded by a noble hound, they decide to whom to bless their virtues. Above him, the Maid of Erin, the spirit of the Irish, leads the people along the frieze, towards liberty, and above her, at forty feet, Daniel O'Connell stands on top the cornice.

The monument stands both in memory of a man and a reminder of the violent road to freedom as even the angels are peppered with bullets and the Maid blood-stained.

Colin starts his walk along the Quay and alone hears Thom Yorke's soft, distant voice. Entranced, the voice haunts and guides his steps:

> *That there, that's not me*
> *I go where I please*
> *I walk through walls, I float down the Liffey*
> *I'm not here, this isn't happening*[1]

The Liffey, An Ruirthech, the Fast Runner, they called it centuries before. The river feeds millions, the people and the industry of the city owe An Ruirthech their lives and livelihood, as it flows through and escapes from the land. Colin knows the Liffey is how he will disappear completely.

He walks away from the heavy flow of traffic along the bridge, not wanting a guard's hassle tonight. One block up is a chapel. He avoids God and walks right along Bachelors Walk. The snow melt soaks into his leather shoes. Cobbled twice, the shoes are in need of repair. The welt and sole are heavily glued and patched and the strings do not match. Still, a day or two of sobriety is too heavy a cost for the fix.

A haze off the river fills the streets with a ghostly fog, fingering out into the rows, lanes, ways, and streets. He passes a small pub and a drunk staggers through the tavern door and the calm breaks, a casus belli. The hot air within and cold air outside twist and turn and

---

[1] "How to Disappear Completely." by Radiohead. On Kid A. Oxford, England. Parlophone Records. Capital Records. October 2000.

become a front, another weathered battle in a timeless struggle. Inside, the war cry blasts from cracked, broken speakers.

Bum. Bum. Bum.

Colin walks west along the quay as if trying to avoid tomorrow's sun. The evening prior, he stashed his bag in Phoenix Park tucked under a thicket rowed by Bachelor's Buttons. Tomorrow he will sleep tucked, as his bag through the night, beneath the bush.

He finds his meal, half a sandwich, on top of a bin outside a Supermac's at the Ha'Penny Bridge. He takes a bite. The Irish pride themselves on their beef though Supermac is trash be it from the grill or from the bin. The burger is soft. The lettuce, onion and tomato are wet and cold. Frozen too long, the burger tastes slightly acidic and metallic; still, he is grateful it has not been in the trash long enough to freeze again. Only the bun is slightly frosted, and the tiny frozen water specks glitter under the light of a streetlamp. *Fries would be nice,* he thinks and crosses the Quay and tosses the wrapper back into a bin on the far side.

He finishes the whiskey. Broke and dry, he circles back to The Lizard, a bar in Trinity, the trendy, touristy part of town. It is a feeding ground for older men to relive their prime and seduce young guys with their wads. Cash flies. Men come, men go. Dim-lit brass chandeliers smear the room in a golden glow. The room is swollen and the music from the dance floor above pounds. The provocative, avantgarde Velvet Underground mixes with the progressive house music of Armin van Buuren. The bass lulls and beats, and the instrumentals and vocals drug him. Spellbound, he is pulled along the dark stained bar by the need for a drink. Sweat and sex seep through the dance floor above and steam the air below. Men drinking watered down vodka stare at him and undress him through gold rimmed glasses and behind blacked out goggles.

Near the end of the room, an older, potbellied man takes off his silver aviators for a better look. He is balding and wears a dark leather jacket and darker collared shirt that clings to the fat underneath. The man shuffles from the stool, hobbles behind it, then offers the seat to Colin.

Colin knows this is the only seat in the place but to think it is a free spot would be wrong. Still, he takes the seat and is glad for the small bit of space between him and everyone else. He leaves his jacket on. He does not intend to stay long but the heat forces his cap off. He tucks it deep into his pocket, too often he has left a place missing a few things.

The fat man leans in close, closer than one needs to speak over the noise, and asks, "Can I buy you a drink?"

He smells foul, almost putrid. His breath tastes of rot.

"Double whiskey, straight."

"A straight kind of guy," the man says and smirks at his assumed cunning. His teeth are stained and the corners of his lips twitch as the weak muscles strain to hold the fat cheeks, rosy from the booze, the curtain call for tonight's entertainment.

Colin has been here before. He has heard that line here before. On cold nights he often comes here for free drinks. The men think he is an easy squeeze, a vagabond, who does not care what people think or ask of him as long as the drinks come; that, and, without a shave or proper shower, he still draws attention. Plus, the bar is kept intentionally dark, no one really wants to be seen here.

A barkeep spots the two.

"Hey Colin, good to see you. What'll it be?"

A rag towel hangs from the back, left pocket of the barman's black jeans. A black and blue flannel outlines a once athletic frame and curly black hair hides yellow eyes. His body is losing to the disease and above the nasally voice of Lou Reed is heard:

> *I am tired, I am weary*
> *I could sleep for a thousand years*
> *Different colors made of tears*[2]

"Hey Jonny. Double whiskey," Colin answers then tilts his head towards the older man. "His tab."

Jonny pours the drinks then tells the older man, "That'll be twelve."

Colin picks up the whiskey, the glass is warm and soap dots the inside. He drinks it and asks Jonny for another.

"Preferably without the soap."

"You're lucky I even have a glass, you dick, you see how slammed I am."

Jonny refills the glass, turns to the wad of cash, and updates the price.

"Twenty-four."

"Right. A slugger are ye?" The balding man remarks and puts a twenty and four coins on the bar.

"In America we tip," Colin tells the man and nods towards Jonny.

"We're not in America."

He flicks his head up towards Jonny again. The man tosses out another euro.

"Twenty-percent."

---

[2] "Venus in Furs" by the Velvet Underground. On *The Velvet Underground & Nico*. Hollywood, California. Verve Records. March 1967.

The fat man takes his wallet from his back-left pocket, pulls out a five note and tosses it towards Jonny. The note slides off the bar and floats into a drop sink. Jonny is appreciative for the extra coin and Colin knows he'll get a few drinks, *on the house*, out of it.

"So it's Colin, eh? I'm Richard," the man says. His disingenuous smile turns carnal.

Colin throws back the second glass, stands to leave and without looking at Richard tells him, "I need a smoke."

He thanks Jonny for the drinks and walks outside. Richard waddles and follows. Outside The Lizard swarms. Men talk and laugh and seduce and swoon in a cloud of smoke. The tobacco is astringent, spice and caramel and menthol wash the air, and patrons clean of the seedier smells picked up inside.

Across from the crowd, a duo of small mannequins in "This Year's New Spring Fashions" are set in the window of a clothing shop. One kid wears a dark blue and white striped shirt and white pants and holds a shovel. Another wears a dress striped the same and is holding a pale. Steel metal grates shield the shop windows and imprison the still children in their work. Soon some parents will come and buy the clothes.

The whiskey kicks, Colin can feel his fingers warming with each drag and wonders if a naked mannequin is finally free or simply out of work. Richard interrupts the thought.

"First time at The Lizard?"

Colin shakes his head, tosses his half-smoked cigarette, steps past Richard and turns to go inside.

"You lettin' on?" Richards asks and blocks Colin path.

"No. You just bore me," Colin answers. "You're all guff. There's twenty other guys in there that'll buy me a drink, eighteen of them look better, and at least ten learned to speak proper English. You want something, speak. In your words, pull your socks up."

"A hundred. My place."

"You skawly . . ."

"Fine. Three."

"Where do you live?"

"Smithfield."

"Show me."

The streets are dark, the night is at its peak. They walk west, down Dame Street. The clock chimes from the gable a top Callagan House, a late 19th Century, red-brick mansion, and the colossal noise from the all hours club, the King George, are heard. They smoke and walk. East of Grattan Bridge and north of the Quay, they turn down a small caliginous alley. Other than a few dumpsters where the well-off tenants, who in the apartments above pay an overpriced rate for an underwhelming view, toss their trash, the alley is empty. Next to a dumpster, Colin notices a shoelace undone. He stops, bends to tie it, and, again, asks to see the cash. It is then, as Richard reaches inside the breast of his jacket, that Colin sees the gun and he slips into memory. Like the steps that led him to the feet of Ireland's liberator, Colin does not think, instead, he forgets the untied lace. He forgets where he is. He falls into the past. To his right is a piece of a pipe, a broken leg from one of the dumpsters, he grabs it and smashes the steel pipe into the side of Richards head.

Death, the final goodbye, the long night, the eternal sleep, the eventual freedom, binds man in its certainty. But in the shrouds of death, there is only uncertainty, and, from this uncertainty, comes the debate and the question of the finality one finds in death. Some have learned to fear death while others have learned to worship it. Some long for it while others run from it. Many, in their final moments, when they are put to the barrel or they stand before the tunnel, ask what worth they leave behind. For some it is the acts in their lives that they wish remembered, for others it is the act of their deaths. Sadly, while both want to stand immemorial, very few in death are glorified. Too often, in those final moments, people fight, cry, and scream in fear or they ignore their fear and in denial cling to a false hope. While a few smile and close their eyes in awe of what is next or find their souls in their last gasp, many others slip away in silence and are found by a smell. Death is certain but men still ask what purpose does death serve? They ask, *why?* The reasons for this question are more varied than the causes of death. Loved ones will question the value of a death and ask why in the death of another do they feel death of self? Tabloids will sensationalize a death and will print a dozen conflicting stories to create a drama around the tragedy. Police will find motive. Priests will find purpose. Each wants to answer the elusive, the ethereal, why? *Why did they have to die?*

But the only truth most will come to understand is how a person died and, to the living, to Colin, how is much more valuable than why. The cause is the most important. When people understand how the dead died, they understand death a bit more, they learn to spot it, and then hide from it.

Colin knows how to keep himself alive because he knows how to kill Richard. Knowledge of both from times before. Still murderer they will scream when they find the left side of Richard's skull fractured between the eye and ear.

> *Ten pints of blood per human, ain't no refills . . .*

It is a pathetic death. One moment Richard stands in the street with a hard on, the next he is on his knees. With his head bashed, the curtain falls. His fat cheeks sag no longer tense behind a cocked smiled. Then his knees give out and the body drops to the pavement.

The body, the dough, it rolls. The jacket opens and the guns slides free. *Sig Sauer P220* is engraved on the slide.

> ... *Take a life, lethal injection or free will* ...

The dumpster leg and Richard's wallet, now empty, *he had the cash,* are tossed into the Quay as Colin walks to the park and leaves Richard fully loaded, dead in the street to lust after the angels.

> ... *Open a book and turn that page, it reads* ...
> *Murder, murder, murder, murder*[3]

---

[3] "Murder," by Game ft. Kendrick Lamar & Scarface. On *Sunday Service* Mixtape. December 2012.

Now

Rose

Rose wakes in a thicket surrounded by Bachelor's Buttons in the north-west part of Phoenix Park, a large open space to the west of Dublin. She and Colin have slept there the past nights. The thicket is old, the ground underneath dry and worn. Bodies have rubbed the grass free. The ground is now a smooth, level earthen bed. At the edges of the small clearing, the thicket is littered, both animals by their leavings and men by theirs have made this place home before. Colin chose the Button from a sing-song she tuned before, when they had first walked through the park.

> *Alone with a Bachelor's Button*
> *Away from it all, how wanton*
> *To hide, to sleep,*
> *Oh so deep*
> *Well, that was quite sudden*

It is a schoolgirl's rhyme, something she knew from before. She does not remember reciting it, she does not remember the walk. Now *let's take a walk* is the walk home when before *let's take a walk* was a chance to get out. Now the walk is the nightly commute. The *in the name of all that is holy, move, the light is green* commute home. The nostalgia and the scenery are lost in the routine and the mundane. The patch in the Buttons is a cheap hostel with bed bugs and shite plumbing.

"We'll leave tomorrow," Colin told Rose before he left for the night.

She found it easier to sleep face up, back flat on the dirt then walk with him. He would walk the streets, bewitched, soul sold to the

Doctor, till the booze wore off or forced him to lie down. He had told her that men hid in the smile and nod and wave and talk during the day. He had told her, "Lights hide, shadows reveal," *or, some cliché like that.* When before, she had laughed and pictured one of the old-time cartoons where the shadows take different forms and silently stalk the unknown casters. Now she could hardly tell the difference between the shadow and the caster, unsure of who is haunted and who is haunting.

The sun slowly warms the night's frost and a slow wind blows the leaves. Before Rose thought leaves shed water every morning like a dog does after a bath, excited, crisp and clean. Now she knows the morning dew will sit and stain the day until the sun heat pulls it from the leaves and ground, from the green sepals protecting the blue pedals as they wait for spring, and from her cold, frost-covered blanket, hat, nose and gloves. She stirs and stretches, keeping her feet tucked under the blanket, to shake the cold, and sees a man walk next to the southern face of the rain-washed wall that runs north of the thicket. It is too early to be a groundskeeper and too late for a random drunk searching for a home.

"Where were you?" Rose asks as Colin takes a seat next to her. Too tired to be angry or annoyed, the frustration leaves her voice as she yawns, "I was worried."

Rose knows his habits and even for Colin this is late. She is not mad because she is no longer worried. But she was worried. Before she had too many people to care for to worry about a single man. Now he is her sole care and when she cannot care for him, she worries. And, on some nights, when she thinks of before, she realizes how it is now her fault she needs Colin. She has become needy.

She acts like a politician, a celebrity, a late-night TV shopper, an alcoholic and a junky. She no longer takes what she needs but must wait to be given her fix. Like a toddler who screams for attention, *pick me, pick me, pick me,* or a junky who finishes the stash before the party starts, like a politician that needs votes, a celebrity that needs fans, and a late night shopper that needs things, stuff, trash. Rose needs, she is dependent on him, but this dependency is irrational.

Rose needs Colin, not for strength, support, or money, she needs him because without him she has no sense of self. Her life is to give and in that she finds what she needs so she stays with Colin in the belief that this keeps her true to who she is. With him, by caring for him, she finds familiarity, she finds a sense of self from before. Yet, politicians lie to get votes. Celebrities leak sex tapes and drunken videos to get attention. Retirees spend their medical money. Junkies steal from their dealers. Her life is misguided and in disorder.

> *I've been waiting for a guide to come and take me by the hand,*
> *Could these sensations make me feel the pleasures of a normal man*[4]

. . .

For a better part of a decade, Rose lived a split life. Half here in Dublin and half someplace else. When in Dublin, she was a surgical nurse at Mater Misericordiae Hospital. When not in Dublin, she worked in understaffed and underfunded clinics around the world. The first few summers were spent working in large metropolitan areas in relative safety, treating diabetes, cataracts, IBS. On occasion she would assist in an emergency, sticking a bullet hole or wrapping a burn victim and, after a while, she found comfort in the chaos. To her colleagues back home, she was known as a trauma junkie and some, the young, inexperienced and over-confident doctors, would make barbs at her whenever she came back to the hospital. In guise of a jest, before a routine operation, resetting a dislocated shoulder or pulling glass from a hand, they would mock, *Get Nurse Rose . . . I'm not sure what to do . . . I've never seen this before . . . Help, please!* or some other adolescent jibe.

These new doctors were insecure and feared a loss of respect towards their assumed status because of Rose's experience. They

---

[4] "Disorder," by Joy Division. On *Unknown Pleasures*. Stockport, England. Factory Records. June 1979

knew she had worked in places well outside the comforts they would never leave. She had treated patients after an overcrowded chicken bus was swept off the road in a mudslide in Peru. In a pop-up hospital after a tsunami devastated Papua New Guinea, she had amputated the leg of a kid run over by an aid truck. One of her favorite stories was when she delivered a baby in the back of a Toyota flatbed as it drove uphill in the pouring rain. It was in Botswana when she was working in a remote clinic in the bush. The mother was young and this was her first baby. The mother terrified, demanded to be taken to the hospital. It was a long drive and a short labor. In that same, remote village in Botswana was the one story she held to herself, the story she reminded herself of under the bushes in Phoenix Park, when she began to pity her life. Rose had come to help those affected by a famine. There she had watched as mothers starved themselves to feed their children. Here a mother had to decide whether to eat in order to feed her still nursing infant or let that child die in order to feed her other children with her own food. *Does it really matter? Was there really much of a choice?* These questions she could not escape, these question kept her awake.

Her stories intimidated the young doctors so they asserted their say-so over the order of things. They reminded Rose, that when in Ireland, she was a nurse and they were the doctors because they knew in the field, in the remote places of the world too often forgotten, where a degree meant little, Rose was a doctor. This fear was petty and naïve. The senior doctors knew it. They knew Rose was a professional, her job was to assist, and when these new surgeons lost their nerve, Rose was there to assure them. She became invaluable in those moments and the fresh, overconfident doctors were humbled and thankful. They learned Rose would always assist them because her life was to serve.

Rose had chosen to be a nurse. She had turned down a doctoral program to be like her mother. Her mother shared stories of patching men, women and children pulled from IRA bombings or freedom attacks, and, even though the deep, unseen scars of this fight for independence cut her mother like the cliffs of the western shores, her mother always spoke of these chaotic times passionately and fondly. Her mother shared stories of how doctors barked orders like the generals of old and how the nurses like the foot soldiers, the enlisted, carried out these orders in blind faith. Rose knew she could take commands but was slow to order them. She had always been one to follow. She enjoyed following. Her father often told her, "Rosie, people use roads because they are easier to walk on and you know they take you somewhere."

She had lived her life as a passenger, helping to navigate, but never as the driver. The one decision she had made, that was truly her own, was to become a nurse so she could take commands when the orders came.

And, so, needing to be led, she follows.

. . .

"I'm fine. No need to worry," Colin tells Rose.

"Where were you though? You haven't walked the night through for months."

"I went by the Lizard and got some money."

Colin hands Rose roughly two hundred, mostly twenties and tens.

She begins to ask and he shakes his head.

Don't.

BEFORE

ROSE

Rarely had she pressed him for answers. She knew the headlines. Most times, those were enough. Still, she had, when needed. It was the fifth or sixth time he had stayed with her in Dublin. Like all the other times, he showed up for a few days, a week at most, then he left. Still she enjoyed his company however short. They found a needed comfort in the other. Her experiences, the joys of her work and the pain it brought, isolated her from her old life. Old friends, old family and old flings, did not understand what kept her separate from them because they were no longer able to relate to her. She had split her life, half here, half somewhere else. Before Dublin was home but, at some point, home had become the other places. Now she wandered between the hours at the hospital and, with Colin, she had found someone to wander with. They understood the others' sense of loss even when they did not understand their own. This allowed them to forget about themselves and find comfort in guiding the other. But eventually, always, Colin remembered, and he left before this comfort became routine.

After one stay, she noticed her bottle of Nembutal was missing. It was an old prescription, prescribed to her when she could not sleep after Botswana. She took it a few times, but the effects were too heavy. She had kept the bottle in case of a bad night, a night she could not escape her memories, when her two options would be to suffer or to sleep. When she noticed it missing, Rose knew Colin took it and was terrified what he might do. She looked for him and found him in a local haunt. It was a worn place, a basement bar on the outskirts of town. The bar stools were cracked, and the couches were stained and torn. Underlit, it was always dark inside, regardless of the time of day. The stale beer and bleach in the air were tangible and masked the fouler, more subtle smells. In the back, there was a little stage where confessions were held. Here the drunks at the bar would sit and listen and watch as the hurting bled.

> *I know I'm getting nowhere*
> *And all the deeds of yesterdays*
> *Have really helped to pave my way*[5]

She sat down and ordered a bottle of beer. After the general, *how have you been*, she asked, "Did you take pills from my house?"

"Yes," he answered. He was not drunk, it was still too early for that, but the straight-forward answer startled her. He rarely admitted anything, instead, he would often sit in silence, as if he had not heard the question, and wait for the question to pass.

"Why?"

"I needed some cash."

"You sold them?" Worry turned to anger. She was pissed. "Do you know what'll happen to me if people find my pills are being sold? You risked my job, my life, for a drunk! What is your problem?"

"They were prescribed over a year ago and you haven't taken one in months."

"So you've been counting my pills? Waiting to make sure I wouldn't miss them? How long have you been waiting to sell them so you can buy a buzz?"

"I didn't sell them. Take'em back if you're worried. I only used two."

---

[5] "Watch Me Bleed," by Tears for Fears. On *The Hurting*. England. Mercury Records. Phonogram Records. March 1983.

He pulled a small orange bottle from his jacket and handed it to her. The label had been taken off.

"I don't understand. Why'd you steal the pills? You didn't take them. You didn't sell them."

"I needed some cash."

He ordered two more beers, paid cash for them, and did not offer any more of an explanation, so she waited. He finished his beer and ordered another. After a while he got up to have a smoke and she followed.

The night had begun. Men were walking home after *drinks with the boys* and Rose understood why Colin tended to drink in this part of town. It was old, industrial, and struggling. The people here wanted something, but they could never tell what that thing was. Rose felt this want. She saw it in the slow walk of these men as another day ended. They wanted tomorrow but were stuck in today.

On the stage a woman covered Band of Horses' "Slow Cruel Hand of Time."

> *Stuck in neighborhoods where everything stopped*
> *It still looks the same*

Next to the cracked cellar windows, Rose heard the confession. Before, Ben Bridwell's soft melodic twang sounded of remembrance, of a boyish want for yesterday. That day, the frontman's voice was replaced with a deeper sound, scratched and broken and feminine. The singer picked at her guitar with force and passed her pain through the strings. She took the familiar story and made it her own. A sad song that she internalized into own torture. The confession was slow and driven. It was an anthem.

. . . The slow cruel hand of time[6]

"Sorry," Colin told Rose after he lit a cigarette. "A while back, I took a pill to sleep. I was asleep in minutes, so I took the bottle."

"You said you took them because you needed money. Where'd the two pills go?"

"I took one, I told you. Someone else took the other."

"So, you sold it?"

"No."

"Colin, I need you to tell me what happened."

---

[6] "Slow Cruel Hand of Time," by Band of Horses. On *Mirage Rock*. Hollywood, California. Columbia Records. September 2012.

COLIN

A few weeks earlier, Colin got off the streets for a few nights and rented a bed in a room with twenty-three other people. It had rained for days and he was too dirty to be let into any bar, so he cleaned up. He paid in cash. Then, after he showered and with a clean pair of socks, he went to bar a few blocks away. It was nothing special. The drinks were not cheap but at least they were not weak. Top 40's hits played, Kanye, Consequence, and Cam'ron, and men casually dressed, talked business. Near last call, a guy in a United cap bought Colin a drink.

How we out in Europe, spendin' Euros.[7]

"Thanks," Colin told him, finished the beer, left and was gone.

He woke up disoriented in the alley behind the hostel. His head ached. It was not from over drinking. The money he carried was gone and his jacket was missing. He did not care. This was not the first time he had been robbed and past experiences had taught him to keep his essentials safe. He did not live anywhere but he did keep a long-term storage locker. In it was his passport, wallet, and nearly all his cash. He could always get more money and the jacket could be replaced at any secondhand shop. He went back to the hostel and slept off the drugs. That night, he changed more than just his socks and went out to a bar frequented by the older gay crowd. He hoped his story would get him a few free drinks.

"So, you're looking to make some money?" asked a man in a Hawaiian shirt and cut off jean shorts. He was well built, with a body

---

[7] "Gone," by Kanye West ft. Consequence, and Cam'ron. On *Late Registration*. Hollywood, California and New York City, New York. Def Jam Records and Roc-A-Fella Records. August 2005.

younger than his face, and was well groomed with short silver hair and a long beard that matched. An ocean, earth, and sky tattoo sleeved his right arm and small, hollow, steel tubes, two millimeters or so across, gauged his ears.

"What's your idea?" Colin asked and drank the beer the man had bought him. Colin had just shared his story and, although he was familiar with the implication, it was always best to know the details of such proposals, indecent or not.

"Let's see how tonight goes, but tomorrow you'll have two-hundred to spend how you'd like."

"Thanks, but you no."

Colin did use these men, for a few drinks, but he did not lead them on. Whenever asked, he said no, *not interested*, but he did always wait for the question. At times, he almost felt guilty then he got drunk. Still, to Colin these bar offered more than a few free drinks. Late into a long and cold night, when the regulars sat and drank in quiet, the place was sad. Unlike the Lizard, this bar was not a butcher shop where men browsed the fresh cuts.

The bar was dark, gloomy, quiet. The music was low, the lights just bright enough. It was a place for the lonely. It was a place for the outcasts, the secluded, the misunderstood, and the misrepresented. Men sat and drank and remembered past love, the love that could not be, and the love that never was. This place was a place of escape, a place to be true to self. Where most came to be accepted and to feel loved, Colin came to be alone and to escape in his thoughts. Here Colin escaped into his grief, he let it overtake him, he could freely and openly be broken, and people did not ask anything of him.

The man was not dejected or offended. It was a quick idea with a needed assumption, and he did not care that Colin had made that assumption nor that he had said no. Colin and the gentleman, of sorts, continued to talk and to drink. The money seemed more of a kindness anyways, the man was gorgeous and charming. He did not need to pay.

"Dean."

"Colin."

The conversation was unforced and, mostly, they talked music. The man, Dean, had been the lead guitarist in some New Wave group Colin had never heard of and, apparently, David Evans and he had bought the same style guitar in the same guitar shop in New York City.

"1976 Gibson Explorer at Stuyvesant Music. Best $250 I've spent, and I still love that guitar. Crazy futuristic. The perfect guitar for the 80's with that mashed Z shape and long neck. It's straight out of some dystopian, future world. Mine was black with a white pick guard, David's was natural wood with the same pick guard. Sure, I bought it a year before him, not that anyone will ever care, nor will anyone want to buy mine for a quarter of a million."

"Sold it for charity, right?"

"Spot on."

A few years before, David Evans, the guitarist for U2, known by his stage name The Edge, sold his signature guitar to raise money for Hurricane Katrina victims. Colin had seen the article in a framed newspaper in a music hall in New Orleans. He had been there on work.

Then they argued hip hop, specifically the undying Queens vs Brooklyn debate.

". . . . Queens reigns over the NYC hip hop game. Nas. Done."

"Brooklyn. Biggie, Jay-Z . . ."

"No, no. no. Check it. Old School Queens has Run DMC and Tribe Called Quest. Then there's Ja Rule and 50. Now Action Bronson and Nicki Minaj have changed the game."

"Very solid but I think you're forgetting about Gang Starr and Dead Prez. Plus, Brooklyn has given us Talib Kweli and Mos Def and the fast talking Busta and ODB. Papoose! Come on."

"Ladies Love . . . "

"I guess a queen would know what ladies love."

It was the reason why people paid extra to drink in public—the company and the banter. When the bar closed Dean invited Colin over for a drink. "It's not far," he said. "Plus, I've got an album to settle our earlier debate."

Interested in the drink and glad for the company, Colin agreed. The walk to the apartment was short. It was an old warehouse space converted into six stories of luxury apartments. The building was twentieth century industrial with 90° angles and fire red masonry bricks from top to bottom. Two sets of glass doors framed in iron opened into a spacious and hollow lobby. The decor was minimal with rust painted beams and exposed black duct work.

A bellhop sat at a glass topped round metal desk.

"Night, Jim. He's with me," Dean told the young man behind the desk, who in turn smiled and waved in acknowledgment.
Colin had taken advantage of the free drinks and the booze had started to work. More immediately, the last shot of whiskey had worked, a bit too well. And in the elevator . . . in the apartment . . . Colin blacked out.

En garde, I'll let you try my Wu-Tang style[8]

Colin woke in a soft bed. He was disoriented. His head ached. This time, it was from over drinking. He knew this pain too well. The room was small and bare. There was a white bureau and a white desk. Next to the desk was a guitar, *the guitar*. A few music posters were framed and hung on the wall: Tokyo Olympics, The Atrix, and Soft Clippings. He got out of the bed and found his pants on the chair at the desk. The chair was red, faux leather with a black stripe down the center. He walked to the next room. It was long. At one end there was a balcony. In the near distance, there are two round chimneys striped in red and white. The chimneys were icons, the Poolbeg Stacks as they are locally known. Each at over 200 meters, they were the sixth and seventh tallest structures in Ireland. Colin knew the towers were part of an old power station along the eastern shore of the city. From the distance of the towers, he knew the walk last night was much further than he remembered. At the other end of the room was a kitchen. It was sleek and minimal with stainless steel appliances and white cupboards. Closer to the balcony, along the far wall, were a black couch and two chairs. Across from the chairs was a record player and to the sides of the record player were floor tower speakers. A high-top, glass table with four chairs was tucked under a floating cabinet.

A man, *the man, Dean*, from the night before, sat shirtless drinking coffee in one of the high-top chairs. He wore striped pajama pants and tan loafers. His back and chest were covered in tattoos. They were old and the colors had faded. The tattoos reminded Dean of a past self he was glad to have permanent memories of.

"Morning, there is coffee if you like," he said and sipped his tall mug.

"Thanks."

---

[8] "Bring Da Ruckus," by Wu-Tang Clan. On *Enter the Wu-Tang (36 Chambers)*. New York City, New York. Loud Records. November 1993

Colin found a cup next to the sink. The place was spotless. Very much in contrast to the bar last night or to Colin that morning. He filled the cup twice with water before he filled it with coffee.

"Cream's in the fridge. Whiskey's in the cabinet."

Colin opened the cabinet for the morning's cure while Bobbie Smith's yearning and introspective voice came from the speakers as a record turned.

> *I forget when to move when my mouth is this*
> *Dry and my eyes are bursting hearts into bloodstained sky . . .*

"I doubt you remember last night but, if you're worried, nothing happened. I prefer my partners conscious. So, I gave you the bed and I slept on the couch. Again, don't worry, I sleep on the couch most nights anyways. But since nothing happened, I don't feel obligated to make you breakfast, plus I've gotta get some work done. Anyways, sucks you got robbed. Here's some cash to get you sorted."

Dean put four twenty notes on the counter.

"It's not much but it will get you where you need to be. I need to get the day started, so I'm gonna shower. See ya around Colin."

Dean walked into the other room and shut the door, and Colin heard the water run through pipes overhead. He finished the coffee, left the twenties and pocketed the bottle.

> *. . . Just one more to inspire me*
> *The desire in me to never go home*[9]

That night, Colin passed a guy in a, *in the,* United hat. He followed him to a bar. It was a different bar, in a different part of town, and

---

[9] "Homesick," by The Cure. On *Disintegration*. Oxfordshire, England. Fiction Records. May 1989.

Colin had shaved. He figured the guy would not recognize him, so he made friends. After he drugged the guy with a pill he had stolen from Rose then robbed him.

The money Colin pulled off the man told him that he had not been his only mark

Rose

"Colin," Rose repeated. "I need you to tell to tell me what happened."

He finished his cigarette and lit another.

"You're right, I sold the pill," he lied. "It's how I paid for the drinks."

"Wait, Colin, what? How dare you risk my career, hell, my life! Screw you!"

She left before he could explain and swore to herself, she was done with his *bullshit*. A few weeks later, after wandering alone, she found him again.

Now

Most nights when Colin gets back, he is elsewhere, stuck someplace in his head. Today he is tense and present. He is alert. As if expecting to find something or someone, he turns his eyes back to the path he had only minutes ago walked along. Rose trails his gaze along the wall and, on its far side, hears the increase in traffic along RT 147 as the, *Come on! The light is green! Your car is not a breakfast nook! Why don't you get up earlier to eat!* morning commute begins. She looks towards the north pedestrian gate that leads into the park and follows the path that leads guests south to an old stone tower house. The house is her favorite landmark in the park. Before, a Gregorian house, the home to the British Under Secretary of the Lord Lieutenant, stood where the tower stands. Then, in late seventies, the aristocratic home was torn down. To the surprise of all, buried within the walls and forgotten for centuries, was Ashtown Castle. Now the personal fortress built by peasants for ten pounds for the lord of 1430 again stands naked and alone.

She turns back to Colin, sees small, blood splatter on the sleeve of this jacket, then touches his hand and asks, "Where are your gloves? Your hands are freezing."

"Traded'em. It's fine."

"Why would you trade them?"

He pulls away his hand and pulls out his flask and shakes it.

Still empty.

He looks at her. Her cheeks are pink and her eyes, moments before glassed over in sleep, like her body not wanting to shove off the blankets and admit to the day, are awake and questioning.

He drops his defense. He knows why Rose asks and knows that she wants to feel trusted, useful, needed.

"I'm fine. Really."

"Alright, well, let's get outta here. You owe me a hot shower."

She stands and stretches. She folds the dark blanket and worn yoga mat underneath it. She shoves both into a red track bag, covered in dirt with torn handles, and tucks and zips the cash into security pocket inside the bag. Then she hands Colin her pillow, which he stuffs into his black duffel, and follows him down the back road towards Ashtown Castle.

Her morning routine now finished before she would have left her bedroom.

They walk south through the park. Phoenix Park, or Fionn Uisce, the ancient tongue for clear water, gets its name from its many fresh streams. It is the largest urban park in Europe, twice the size of New York City's Central Park and larger than all the parks in London combined. When new to the park, strangers are entangled in its overlapping and rounding paths. Rose and Colin know the paths and vary their routes to and from to avoid any suspecting eyes. Before long, to the west, Rose sees the Papal Cross. At 115 feet and constructed of white painted steel, the cross, raised only a few decades ago, is in harsh contrast to the greyed old stones of the derelict, centuries old buildings throughout the park. The Cross shines, while the buildings hide.

They exit the park near Magazine Fort, another neglected Irish-English structure that never served its purpose; and, painted on the boarded gates, is a lesson in case someone forgets:

> *Now's here's the proof of Irish sense*
> *Here Irish wit is seen*
> *When nothing's left that's worth defense*
> *We build a Magazine*
> *- J. Swift*

Homeless, bags covered in dirt with sheets that smell of old water and clothes that smell of moss, Rose follows Colin out of the park and into the city. On the southern footpath, they walk east along the Quay. The sun cuts the cold, old air and the new, warm air is felt off the river. Color comes with dawn; it seeps between the greys of the night and breaks the austere morning. Rose does not want to ask, she knows not to ask, but she cannot ignore it as Colin again turns around to check behind them and again she sees the iron-rich red on his light-brown sleeve. Before she thought most of it dirt, but, now in the light, as the colors become distinct, she see that the blood covers him. It cannot be his.

"Colin. . . Colin," repeats Rose. "Your sleeve, that's blood, that's a lot of blood."

Colin stops and opens his duffel, then he takes off his jacket, shoves it into the bag and tosses the duffel back over his right shoulder. He is shaking and quickly clasps his left hand over his right to steady his nerves. He takes a single breath then takes Rose's hand in his left. He squeezes her hand, a that little gesture of assurance calms them both and quiets her.

Colin stops near Ha'Penny Bridge, the Bridge of the Liffey, Droichead na Life, and buys two coffees and a pastry from a street vender, the first, with a bit of cream, he hands to Rose, the second black he keeps. On a small personal speaker comes the Local Natives, the sound of the Californian Sun. Their voices, subtle and calm, an agreement.

> *Hey now, is it the dawn or the end?*

The hours we talked
You wished we'd stopped
Acting like it's nothing at all[10]

At Hackett Bridge, they cross the Quay. It is a newer pedestrian walkway and here Rose feels the city awake. *Its buzz.* Joggers and cyclists speed by in their daily routines and trolleys roll by and carry the first passengers of the day to where they will later come from. Rose smiles. She loves the mornings, the starts, the new days, and she lets go of Colin's *whatever*. Like the jacket, the story and everything she shoves away, hopefully forgotten.

They continue their walk down to Gardiner Street and, a bit north off the river, out of the kumtage, they stop at a cheap hostel. The hostel is in the political heart of Dublin just north of the Teach an Chustaim, an architectural jewel of the Irish built by a Brit and still under restoration after being set on fire nearly a hundred years before. This part of Dublin is known. The neighborhood, the hostel, the rooms have a reputation. It smells of shipwrecks and raids and a few hundred years of shit. It is the mouth of Ireland. It swallows and spews, swallows and spews. Ships come and go. Before refrigeration this part of town stank as all the rot flushed from the country. Now it is classed. Men work here, the privileged stroll. It is here, a block to the east one finds the Mother of Dublin, the Chapel on Marborough Street, the place to find God, a God that caters to the privileged and serves the working man.

The hostel is one of the working man, a converted Georgian House, another something built by the Brits. Its opposite, the Gresham Hotel, two blocks west, on the other side of God, just north of the breeze block on O'Connell, is where the privileged sleep. Colin has cash for both but not the stature for the latter.

---

[10] "I Saw You Close Your Eyes," by the Local Natives. On *Sunlit Youth*. Loma Vista, Infectious, and Hostess Records. September 2016.

They check in with a Rose's driver license and Colin pays cash for three nights and slides the wrinkle-faced owner an extra hundred for the deposit.

"Room 38," the old woman tells them and, as if from a script: "Fair warning, it's a small price on the pocket and another small price on the ears; but, still, it's cozy enough and I can promise it's got clean sheets, warm water, and a roof that does its job."

Two floors up, right down the hall, second door on the right, is Room 38. Colin inserts the key, turns the knob, and opens the door. A bit over halfway the door stops. Jammed behind the door is a cheap off-white, wooden nightstand with three legs and a top. The edge of the door and the top of the nightstand are heavily chipped after countless confrontations. On top of the nightstand is a green lamp, its shade striped in red and white. To the left of the door, the switch. When flicked, the room is lit in a hazy, not quite district red hue. Next to the nightstand is a double bed with white bedding. A white throw pillow with a green four-leaf clover is placed between two white pillows. The space smells of starch and bleach. The west facing window looks down onto Gardiner Street.

Rose is thankful for a bed and, *my God I'm going to drain this place of hot water,* she thinks as she strips down and sprints to the shower. Her jeans and shirt are off before her bag hits the bed. The bag rolls off and joins the jeans, shirt, socks, panties, and bra. Her socks are still white, off white; it had been two weeks since her last laundry day, but the socks were still a single wash away from crisp, clean, and dirt free. Her bra and panties matched, black with white polka dots. The bra is cut low and the knickers are cut offs, boy shorts, nicknamed from the era in sunny California when men cut their pants off to the ass. *Something only a boy would do, peacock around with his ass out,* fathers thought, stupefied by the latest trend. The underwear is laced at the edges to mimic the loose threads that hang from jeans after cut. It is shaped not to hold and hide but to tease and set a mood.

Colin loves the cut. He sees Rose again for the first time this week. Colin wants to love Rose, but he walks with two shadows.

Love me better, kiss me back, love me more . . .

There is someone else with him. He is never alone. The other travelers blend into his single distraction. Some people stay a few days, maybe a week, a quick trip to see another side of life. Most people pass stop only a night or two along their own trail. A few have stayed long enough to see time is the only change. Colin hates this. The worst is when he wakes up and thinks the woman next to him another. She is the only one he ever thinks he wants and not the only one he has lost.

Rose has been with Colin, by him, physically close to him, for years yet most days he is distant, separate and detached, away in his own head somewhere else. But when he is present, he does love her. He is in love with her, infatuated in the dream, the tale, the what if, the could it be, the if we only.

. . . Tuesday afternoon, I ain't got shit to do but fall in love with you[11]

Colin has fallen in love with Rose more times than remembered because he then always forgets. In the hostel, he falls in love with her as he watches her hop in the shower and turn on the faucet not waiting for the water to warm. She shivers and squeals as cold water runs down her back. She is beautiful. The waves of her straw-gold hair, now wet, lay flat against her and take a soft red hue. Her mother had named her Rose because of this and as she aged her hair lightened but every time it gets wet it shows its first color. She stands 5'9" in three-inch heels, *boots preferably*. Her curves scream to be a mother though nature took that dream when cysts took her ovaries. Her skin is milk white, that Irish white that goes red in the smallest sun. Before Colin she was tone, a woman who cared for her body. Now with Colin she is hard, a woman whose care is her body.

---

[11] "II Shadows," by Childish Gambino. On *Because the Internet.* Glassnote Records. December 2013.

When she lost her apartment, Colin asked, "Cancel your gym?"

"You prick! That doesn't matter. You really think fifteen Euros is gonna cover my bills? Don't you think I thought of that?" she huffed, though she had not cancelled it.

After months of unemployment, months of confusion and months of uncertainty, the gym had become her one constant. It was her place to run away worries and she was sure she could always find an extra fifteen euros.

"No," he told her. "You've got a clean bathroom and shower; plus, you've got a locker. Whatever you do, pay your gym fee. Banks can close your accounts, but you can always pay your gym bill in cash."

"Little trick I picked up from a friend," he concluded and raised his glass in a toast to the wisdom of an old friend and polished it off.

It took her a day on the streets to realize the value in this friend's advice.

Back in the hostel with the booze worn off and only mild shakes, Colin starts to undress and moves towards the bed.
"Shit brains if you touch that bed, even look at it, before you wash down, I will put you down."

She smiles, flicking water towards him, and he disarms in exhaustion. Blissfully, they forget everything for the next few hours in sleep and play.

Rose wakes up some hours later. Colin is naked under the sheets, he is lying on his stomach, breathing heavy into the pillow. On the small corner desk, a digital clock shows 2:26 in red blocks. Rose gets out of bed, dresses quickly in only the basics—shoes, pants, shirt, jacket—she does not want to waste time putting on what she will take off soon enough. She spots a twenty note in Colin's pants, takes it, and goes to a corner store. The store is small with only two small aisles lined with the essentials of city life: toilet paper, beer, snacks, a bowl of fruit, and a rack of magazines. *The Sunday Times* cover shows crossed fingers with a headline that reads:

> The Global Economy
> ONE YEAR LATER
> It's been bad . . .

Thanks for the update, she thinks.

She finds a four pack of Prazsky. *Why ever pay for one Budweiser when you can get four for a fiver of something better?* echoes Colin as she grabs the beer. She smiles and hopes he might stay the night.

He can be wonderful, she thinks and pays with the twenty note.

The bill is clean, almost new. She knows not to ask where the money came from, but, still, she worries and wonders, *How did he get this? Why was he covered in blood?*

She exits and buys a döner with the change from a street vendor outside, then heads back.

Rose is gone when Colin wakes. As he lays face down in the bed, he sees a coffee or porter stain on the carpet, he can see where the glass hit the ground and the liquid poured out. The stain, a memory of the drop, the fall, a permanent shadow, is forever seared. He follows the dark lines to where Rose's clothes lie on the ground and the dots of her bra take him.

Before

Colin

"This party, am I right?"

> *I don't care if it's Chinatown or on Riverside. (Where I live).*
> *I don't have any reason. I left them all behind. (Where I'm at).* I'm in a *New York State of Mind*[12]
> *Holding a M-16, with a pen I'm extreme, NOW*[13]

"Damn. Billy Joel and NAS. That'd be a great show," Isaac yelled over the remix.

"Yep," Colin agreed and tapped his glass to Isaac's.

The party was another night on top of the world. They were there to celebrate their final semester in graduate school, each a 100K in debt and sipping fifteen-dollar gin and tonics twenty floors up under the glow of the Empire State Building.

As they sat, chatted, and made bold prediction of how they would pay off their debts, Jane, Isaac's fiancée joined. Even in the overcrowded and under lit room, Isaac reached out his hand and found hers. He pulled her close to him and *I can't believe I get to spend my life with you* flashed perfectly and equally between the two of them.

---

[12] "New York State of Mind," by Billy Joel. On *Turnstiles*. Hempstead, New York. Columbia Records. May 1976
[13] "N.Y. State of Mind," by Nas. On *Illmatic*. New York City, New York. Columbia Records. April 1994

Isaac and Jane took the train in, they lived a bit west of the city. Jane was thin with a round face and round vibrant eyes and long wavy hair. Isaac was square with wide shoulders and short puffy hair pushed to the left. They were recently engaged, and their story was as beautiful as it was lucky and fated. They met in high school, before the first football game in their freshman year, Jane made peanut butter chocolate chip brownies for her crush on the team. She asked a friend for the boy's address and her mother drove her to his house. When Isaac answered the door, she asked if this other kid, her crush, was home. Isaac told her no and asked why she thought this other guy would be at his house. Jane too embarrassed not to lie, handed him the plate and told him she just wanted to make sure none of his friends were there to eat the brownies. Isaac, never one to miss an opportunity, asked Jane on the spot to be his homecoming date and Jane, stuck in her lie, could not refuse. The night of the dance they fell into the infatuate love of youth then, after a few months, she told him the truth that the brownies were not for him, and, ever the charmer, Isaac told Jane he would always be glad to be her mistake but next time no peanuts. A decade later, they've grown together as only young lovers do. They learned to be individuals through their intimacy with their wants, values, needs, and goals shared. It was when together they were singularly fulfilled.

Fate can be beautiful.

"I have a friend I'd like you to meet," Jane told Colin. "She went to college with me and lives in Jersey with her parents. She's attending Rutgers's Law School in the fall."

Smart and friends with soon to be Mrs. Jane W, thought Colin.

"Thanks, but right now, I really don't have time. Two apps are in development that I need to find some cash for if I ever want to pay off these ridiculous loans and credit cards," he said and sipped his gin and tonic. "I mean I barely have enough time to pretend to water my fake plants."

Cheers Mitch.

"Because a woman starting law school wants a man who is always around. She's cool and, honestly, needs to get out of the house a bit more. I mean she moved back home. Surely you could help her find somewhere else to stay occasionally."
"Yep, my five-room spot with seven people that has a longer train ride than Jersey to get to, is always open to any of your friends."

Colin cheered the air at his shrewdness and drained his g-n-t. "Time for another. Anyone else? Round's on me."

"It would be rude not to," Isaac answered as two other buddies, in unison, lifted their glasses.

He could drink the complimentary vodka given to them by a buddy of Isaac's who promoted the club. The promoter was a European expat living in the City, and it was a stretch to say Isaac and he were friends. They were given the complimentary bottle because they showed up with Jane and a dozen of her friends, so out of a false sense of chivalry Colin believed the woman deserved first dibs at the bottle.

Colin walked from the small, glass-top table at the back of the thin and narrow cocktail lounge. The room was dark, two glass chandeliers stained blood-red twisted out from the ceiling, as if gnarled, crystal trees grew out of the floor above. Gold curtains split sections of the room and gave certain clientele a bit of extra privacy. Plush couches rounded tables, covered with Absolut bottles and half full plastic glasses, sparkled clear, red, and black. None of the couches matched—purple, orange with lime green squares, zebra print—and, between the couches, turquoise foot stools filled the empty spaces. That night, most of the seats were empty as people enjoyed the first taste of spring out on the balcony. It was a Yankee night to make even the Angels jealous. People smoked and talked under the lights of the Empire State Building, red and white tonight in honor of the New York Fire Department.

Colin knew the cocktail server wanted them to order drinks through her. Still he walked to the bar out of instinct or a sense of familiarity, a loyalty to his barman friends. These short-skirted servers walked with hundreds, popping a $650 bottle of champagne a few dozen times a night, while the guys and gals behind the bar hustled for every buck. He knew the waitress was attractive and most of the tip was deserved. Men googled and goggled and sometimes grabbed. Today, the cocktail server has lost her namesake's jacket but kept true to the classic colors. She wore a black tie, sleeveless white button down, halfway unbuttoned to show skin in a money grab, and a tight black skirt that showed her white boy shorts when she leaned just so. *Those alone are almost worth the wait,* he thought.

She was Russian. He thinks she was Russian. She looked Russian. She sounded Russian. *What do I know? She's a hustler. She could be a dude. Hell, I'd do it, money's good enough, wonder if they're hiring?*

The booze had started to work.

The bar was in a side room, perpendicular to the lounge. At sixty feet, it stretched the length of the room. Three bartenders worked in circles. They spoke a language for those who did not have time to repeat the same thing a few hundred times a night to the hundreds of people that crowded the bar and ordered drinks.

A bartender pointed to Colin. "Four gin and tonics," Colin shouted over Public Enemy and Benny Benassi.

In sync, elbows dropped as liquor poured and the beat kicked.

> *Bring the Noooiiisssseee*
> *Bass! How low can you go*[14]

---

[14] "Bring the Noise," by Public Enemy. On *It Takes a Nation of Millions to Hold Us Back*. New York City and Long Island, New York. Def Jam Records and Columbia Records. June 1988.

The bartender nodded then pointed to the women on Colin's left as he filled ten glasses with ice.

"Two vodka Redbulls. What type of vodka do you have?" asked the woman.

The bartender picked up a bottle of Jack in his right hand and a bottle of Absolut in his left. He filled the far two glasses to the right with Jack and the four glasses to his left with Absolut.

"This and those."

He flashed the woman the bottle of Absolut then flicked it towards the liquor shelf behind him.

"Okay, Absolut."

He was a gunslinger. The time the Irish four-count ended in the second glass of Jack, a bottle of Bacardi was in his hand and filled the next three glasses. The Absolut bottle was placed back on the speed rack and Bombay filled the final glass. Glasses filled, he pointed the bottle of Bombay at a customer further down, in the universal barman's sign for *what do you want?*

"Mitcher's Rye, double, little ice," Colin heard over the speakers.

The barkeep grabbed credit cards from the three guys with the last ten drinks. In a single act, he stretched between the computer on the back bar and the drink station. He swiped the cards with his left and topped off drinks with the soda gun—water, soda, soda, cranberry, tonic, coke, ginger, ginger, ginger, diet coke—with his right, while he dodged the other two bartenders and barback as they ran up and down the bar aisle in a mad grab at everything. He tossed the drinks and tabs to the paid-out customers down the bar then filled another ten glasses with ice. The tenth glass was a smaller, rocks glass.

The bartender winked towards the woman who ordered the Mitcher's, poured it first, then told the lady, "You first for ordering a proper drink. That'll be $28."

Colin knew she was stunning. Bartenders saw people every day and anyone who watched this man work knew he was a sharpshooter with the eyes to match any profession. Law men were given targets, bartenders found theirs. When a bartender paid a complement and, it was not a money grab, it was true. Colin turned his head, this was not a money grab. The woman stood at 5'3 and wore a black dress with white polka dots. Her hair was black, then brown when security shined a light towards a drunk at the other end of the bar.

"What do you mean, 'You're not comfortable with me paying for another drink?'" the drunk screamed at one of the staff behind the bar. "Do you know how much I spent! Hey, hey, hey, I'm talking to you."

The staff member ignored the drunk man's shouts, glanced at security and nodded her head toward the man.

Colin was glad for the quick light. When her hair lightened, it reminded him of dark chocolate, *Hersey's Kisses dark chocolate*, the kind his grandfather kept in his pocket mid-winter. He heard his grandfather's voice, *when my chocolate feels like toffee or I can't gum my gummies, I know it's time for change*. His grandfather had different candies for each season: toffees for spring, gummies for summer, hard candies for fall, and chocolate for winter.

He thought Israeli from the curls. That and they were in New York City. He learned she was a second generation American. Her grandparents were Basque and Lithuanian.

She was beautiful.

"I know you have one, but can I buy you a drink?" Colin asked.

She looked at him with mild interest and tossed $35 on the bar.

For a woman at a bar, "Can I buy you a drink?" was asked more than "How are you?" And, she could not even remember when someone asked her, her name before asking to get her drunk. To her Colin was just another guy in another bar.

"Not now but after this one," he explained. "If I'm boring or rude or obnoxious, walk away, or just wait for the drink, then walk away before you find out I'm boring or rude or obnoxious. I won't protest. But, I could be funny, possibly even clever. I've never been called clever but who knows. I obviously don't."

He was nervous so he talked. He was scared he would say something stupid, but he knew his regret would last all night if he said nothing, while his shame would only last until the end of the next drink. He hoped she would give him a chance to prove that he was not of a singular mind.

"Thanks. Maybe later," she answered. "I just got here, and my friends are looking for me. I think they have a table in the back."

She had a presence that was concrete but not forced. She was calm and patient in the restless crowd and she was kind enough to acknowledge him.

The barkeep grabbed the cash. "It's all yours," she told him and walked towards the back.

"At least let me part the sea of drunks for you," Colin asked. "My friends have the last table, break free of me whenever you find yours, and that drink is available until two. 'Nothing good ever happens after two,'" he said in a terrible imitation.

Nixon . . . Clinton . . . Costas?

"Okay," she replied and nodded ceremoniously.

"Words of my father and strangely they ring true more by the day. But let's not bring up my father, you'll have to buy me a drink for that."

She smiled. It was genuine and, in a city of 8 million, where people were guarded and do not often share their joy, a genuine smile was a special gift.

In this city, as in too many other places, people wore headphones and talked to others miles away to avoid the person next to them. They hid in the comfort of their own familiarity because they did not know, nor wanted to know, the lives of their neighbors. Men and woman tucked themselves into the blankets of modern convenience to hide their joy and hide from the pain of others. Joy was not shared and pain was too relatable. In a subway car, a man could stand and share his blight, *I'm homeless and haven't eaten in three days because I'm a heroin addict who just got out of jail after I stole and sold bikes locked outside of a school,* and people could identity with his troubles even if the excuse of the man was not justifiable in the minds of the listeners. People identified with the pain of not having a home or being hungry regardless if the pain was self-inflicted. The pain was shared through transposition. People gave a dollar to a homeless man to ease their pain as they passed the next twenty. It was impossible not to feel the pain of another because everyone suffers. Joy was much harder to share although much more needed. A man cannot stand and share his joy, *I bought a new house for my wife and kids, where I put full meals on the table, and I am now on the way to a job that gives me a sense of satisfaction, oh, and I was recently promoted,* with universal understanding. It took a very special, very selfless person to find joy in this, if they had none of it. How can someone with nothing share in this joy? How can someone who has forgotten what joy feels like share in the joy of another?

Colin was embraced in her smile.

It was beautiful.

"What's your name?" he asked.

"Fifty-two," interrupted the bartender and slid four gin and tonics towards Colin.

Colin looked at the four glasses and he nodded his head towards the computer and cash box. Earlier that night he opened a tab with the last credit to his name.

"Lukends, Colin."

"Thanks," answered the bartender and turned to the punch in the drinks.

"Well, Colin, I'm Sarah. And, if you leave your tab open, I'll be sure to get that drink even after two."

"Deal." Colin grabbed the drinks and worked his way through the jam-packed room.
You'd think we were in Meatpacking right now, he thought and chuckled at his newly discovered, alcohol induced cleverness.

"Sarah!" Jane screamed over Colin's shoulder. "You made it! And I see you found Colin."

"Yep. We met," Sarah told her then winked at Colin. "He hit on me at the bar."

"You ass. I told you I had a friend for you to meet and you tell me your too busy so what do you do? You try and pick up the first woman you see."

She teased and punched Colin's shoulder.

"Hurt him after he's delivered my booze," Isaac pleaded and took his drink.

"Whatever I told you, I take back," Jane said to Sarah. "He obviously is just another . . ."

"Time Out!" screamed the waitress as she waved a sparkler and placed another bottle on the table.

Saved by the Bottle: A Grownup Zach Morris Tale

"Let's get drunk!" she shouted, opened the bottle, and poured a drink. "Nostrovia!"

Colin swore he could hear Ludacris in the head of the waitress as she threw back the vodka.

> *Like somebody 'bout to pay ya*
> *Don't worry about them haters*
> *Keep your nose up in the air*[15]

They all drank and the night began to fade.

Watch our stuff were the last words Colin remembered from Jane as she dragged Sarah and the girls off to dance.
"At least we get the bottle," a buddy pointed out, Colin cannot remember who, and poured two shots.

They drank then the buddy leaned close, nudged Colin and flicked his nose. "Spanish lessons, you're never done with school my brother," he told him and they walked towards the bathroom.

High and drunk, the night was lost in the lights. The crossfades shadowed the crowd. The music was turned up. The couches were pushed back. Late in the night, Colin walked out onto the balcony for fresh air and a smoke, vodka Redbull in hand.

---

[15] "*Money Maker,*" by Ludacris. On "*Release Therapy.*" Atlanta, Georgia. Disturbing the Peace Records and Def Jam South Records. September 2006

The three C's to a proper New York diet: cigarettes, cocaine, and caffeine.

"Wow. Now that is pathetic," said a familiar voice.

It was Sarah. She had turned from watching the cars below and now eyed his drink. She, like everyone else on the balcony, had stepped outside to momentarily escape the ruckus inside.

"I just really wanted to work out my liver today," Colin replied and shrugged.

"Whiskey or wine is my daily regimen," Sarah answered and shook her glass.

"That's good. But a true drinker knows the key to a good drunk is the tried and true Tony Horton work out, muscle confusion. And everyone knows vodka Redbulls are the DOC, the Drink of Choice, the Denominazione di Origine Controllata of alcoholics. For what you see here is 250% of your daily value worth of B6. I know. Right? Impressive. Now B6 is lost in most of our processed foods so this is a big deal. But it is metabolized through the liver which means it slows down the rate alcohol is metabolized while giving you a jolt of caffeine to keep you up long enough to metabolize it."

The latest bump had kicked.

"Okay, now it is just sad," she said and shook her head ashamed.

"You'll never hear me talk down a drink. Everyone has its place. Would I order this in a pub while I watch the All Blacks massacre a bunch of criminals? Never. But on the top of the world, shadows cast by those lights fifteen hundred feet up at 3:00 in the morning, I'll drink this medieval jet lag juice."

"I thought you'd be home already. Isn't your daddy waiting up to tuck you in?"

"You don't get to talk about my father, you still have yet to buy me a drink."

"Take mine, I can't watch you drink that. It's a real turn off. All I can picture is you grabbing a box of cheap wine, slipping a baseball cap on, backwards, and singing *Don't Stop Believing* in a horrific falsetto."

"My falsetto is divine," Colin took her rocks glass. "I guess I'll have to honor my word and buy you that drink now."

"Another day. The time has passed and the offer is over. Plus, the last train home leaves in less than an hour and your dad's right, nothing good happens after two."

She picked up her handbag, a red weekend bag with dual-top, roll handles and an adjustable cross body strap. She unzipped the top, grabbed a pen from one of the slip pockets inside, then told Colin to give her his arm.

"Why?" he asked, mockingly of course, and extended his right arm, forearm exposed, the sleeve rolled up sometime in the past hours. She wrote her number across the veins, the blood lines of blue now inked over in pink, 908-254-1232.

"Because now you don't have to awkwardly ask Jane for my number or creepily stalk me online. Call me tomorrow."

She kissed his cheek under the lights of the Empire State Building. It was their movie moment, their album cover. Her hands rested on his left forearm, the arm bent at the elbow. Her touch was soft and reliant. She trusted him not to move. He was her support as she leaned onto her toes for that extra inch of height to place a single kiss high on his cheek above the week old beard. He fell in love with her. In a moment they were lovers. They were young and in love ontop of the world. Then they were old with wrinkled faces and life over with only them at the end. In that kiss, a lifetime passed.

Now

As he lies in the cheap sheets on Gardiner Street, Colin does not truly remember the kiss. The silhouette in polka dots and a kiss on the cheek is a washed memory. It is blurred. It is flat. He is angry at the dream broken by time. He is angry at what he cannot remember and lost because of what he has chosen to forget. He is exposed with his memories not lost to time but buried to feeling. He is angry because he cannot remember the joy of that kiss but he cannot remember because he chose to forget the pain of the memory.

A slip of emotion

He cannot remember this kiss and he cannot remember what Sarah looked like on the first night they met, and he blames it on the alcohol and cocaine but he knows this is not true. Half the time out in New York he was drunk and high. It was New York City and he was young. He worked his ass off during the day then partied until he worked again. The insignificant memories, the details and people he met in random rooms on random nights, are clear:

A bum, his face half covered in syphilis pox and a pathetic beard, wheeled a wheelchair onto the train. He was wet and smelled of booze and stale cigarettes and piss. His jacket was faded green and his shoes were surprisingly white, almost new. The bum fell from the chair and lied on the subway. He rolled onto his side, curled his knees towards his chest, and relieved his bladder into a glass liquor bottle pulled from his light brown pants. The bottle overflowed. Piss spilled on the man and car floor. He stuck the bottle back into his jacket and pulled himself back into his chair. The train car slowed and the man then stood. Again, he pulled the bottle from his pants and this time took a swig from it then pushed the wheelchair out of the car.

A mattress has been pulled into the street and eight women lied atop it. All eight are in their late twenties or early thirties and each are dressed in different animal themed pajamas: puppy, shark, monkey, panda, elephant, lion, seal and yellow canary. It was the night before the elephant's thirtieth birthday and she wanted to ring in the new decade under the stars. They brought Colin a bowl of spaghetti and a headband with kitten ears. He gazed at the stars as they mixed with the lights of the city. The Brooklyn Bridge, the skyline, the guided them to towards his dreams.

Red-crystal slippers spasmed in the stall to the left of the urinal in a basement bathroom where he relieved himself. Upstairs was a drag show, he had come to support a buddy who was performing. He looked to the left, the door of the stall was gone, and he saw the hair covered calves and the black Doc Martens with orange soles of a man on his knees. He decided not to flush or wash his hands.

It was early morning and raining. Him and a few thousand other people exited the subway at the 8th Street Station. A man in a light tan suit handed his umbrella to a young girl in a school uniform, khaki shorts and blue polo, and a pink backpack. "Think you might want this," the man hinted to her then smiled, opened a copy of the METRO over his head, and ran into the rain. His suit was dark brown by the next block.

Colin recalls these stories, these facts with none of the human bits of the memories left. He does not remember the smell of the bum, the vile mix of old booze and urine, and he does not remember holding back his vomit. He does not remember the sense of wonder at the lights of the skyscrapers as they mixed with the stars. He does not remember the uncomfortable, awkward, hurried shakes, two exactly, as he quickly finished his business and left the strangers to their subterranean revelry. He does not remember feeling proud of the silly man running down the street with a newspaper over his head. He does not feel the confusion, humor, and pain of walking the City. He does not feel these memories. They are stories, headlines read from the daily paper: *Bum Drank Urine . . . Women Looked Up . . . Person Pleasured . . . Girl Handed Umbrella . . . .*

Before he would laugh and cry when he told these stories, now they are simple facts and are not worth the effort to forget.

But in those rough sheets, in a cheap hostel, in the capital of Ireland, he is angry because it is easier to be angry than to remember. He cannot remember that kiss. He cannot remember the face of the woman who made him the man he is now. If he did remember her, he would then be the man he was before and he would be forced to feel the little human bits, the joy in and the pain from that kiss.
Polka dots,
Myodesopsia,
They float as flies that cannot be touched or waved away
These dots are stuck behind the eyes

Rose returns to the room. Colin is back in the shower. She does not join him. She sits at the small corner table and watches him as he shaves his cheeks, then neck, with the single blade safety razor she found in a throwaway store. It is a new blade that she had used only once. Twice he cuts himself. She watches the blood mix with water and run down his chest and over his scars. The blood trails over his wounds as if they had reopened. At times Colin lies about the scars when others ask about them. At times, the times he forgets and thinks her another, he lies to her about the scars. She knew the lies because she healed the wounds.

BEFORE

ROSE

Rose met Colin bedridden in an underfunded hospital in the murder capital of the world, San Pedro Sula, Honduras. Medics had responded to a call of a male, seemingly dead, in the Cleo Gonzales neighborhood south of the infamous Rivera Hernades district. The call came from a morning crew member of a chicken joint on Calle Principal. The call shocked none of the hospital staff. Calle Principal was the first major road off CA13 from Aeropuerto Ramon Villeda Morales. The call today was another guy beaten for poor decisions and his pocket change. EMTs referred to those calls as *La Mordida de la Perra* coined after the *Warning: Beware of Dog* signs people put on their gates. *No puedo llorar después de que eres un poco,* joked the men as they loaded screaming patients into the ambulance. Most times it was a local dispute. Other times it was an over-confident backpacker, the *I've stayed in a lot worse* traveler who wants to brag to his buddies. Or, it was the naive, the, *there is no way this town is as dangerous as the news makes it, I'll just pop in real quick during my layover and get a bite and maybe a drink,* tourist. The worst was when kids were involved. Parents were easier to control when their children were threatened and acted without thought because of that fear. Sadly, and too often, these kids were left to sit in the hospital with a, *they died saving your life,* eulogy from one of the nurses. No parents should bury a child, yet no child should feel at fault for the death of a parent.

When the medics responded, Rose was in Roatan, a small island and a day's ride north-east from San Pedro Sula, sleeping off her day of margaritas, on her scheduled one week, *get-away from it all,* vacation. She came back two days later and, to her surprise, she heard the rhythmic and mechanical hum of the backup generator. Someone was not willing to take any risks with the patient inside. Then she found the man doped up in Bed 4 of the ICU. She reviewed his chart and found he had several broken ribs and a punctured left lung. Both legs had fractures and his right hand was shattered. Cuts covered his body. Where the plaster casts stopped, cotton bandages started.

The injury that troubled, well annoyed, the nurses most was to his rectum because every move tore open fissures that bled through the bandages. When this happened the nurses had to redress the wound or, in their words, *envolver su culo de nuevo*. The most worrying damage for the doctors was the impact wound to his parietal bone. The doctors hoped there was no brain damage. In most instances, the hospital would airlift a patient with these injuries to a better equipped facility. However, the medical plane was an old twin prop utility aircraft and the doctors would not send a suspected American patient with TBIs to potentially hemorrhage in the unpressurized craft.

tSAH
A balloon lost to the sky by the hands of careless child
The balloon, the veins, will pop,
Will rupture and die

They believed him American due to his black leather Chelsea boots and Calvin Klein shirt, but he carried no ID, and this prevented the doctors from requesting assistance from the US Military at Soto Cano Airbase south of the city. Yet, if he died and was found to be American, the doctors feared USAID would cut its funding to the hospital. They, the doctors, the nurses, the local patients, could only pray and, at the additional expense to the hospital, run the generator at all times.
For ten days they kept him sedated. Colin remembered little, the smell of bleach and glow of florescent lights. He did not remember when the doctors came in, played with the machines around his head, and asked him questions. To each he answered, "No save."

Then they would explain, again, that his head injury likely caused short term memory loss and that his memories would likely come back when he was pulled off the sedatives. He did not remember this. He did not remember the police, the cops in matching black suits that wore boots heavy with authority, or the way the room became tense and unwelcoming when they questioned him. To their questions, he answered the same, "No save."

Then they would explain he had nothing to fear, they would protect him if he told them what happened. After he continued to evade their questions, they told him they knew he was lying to protect himself from drug charges and out of fear of the dealers if he talked.

Colin did not remember this.

Rose did.

He did remember that at some point Rose appeared. She was the doctor who spoke English and did not ask questions he would not or could not answer. Rose, at that time, held very little interest in his story. She was sick of men like him. When the hospital director assigned her the patient, he told her, "If he dies, the hospital will close. If he lives, we'll get a new ward."

To her he was a careless, overprivileged, and inexperienced American man who decided a night of skiing in Honduras would be a fun story and whose decisions put the hospital she loved at risk. Yet, she was vigilant in her duties to him as a patient. Daily she checked his vitals and watched over him. When he became conscious, she asked what he needed. For what he thought was a week and she knew to be twelve days, he said nothing. A few days after being taken off the heavy stuff, *el Captain C,* she brought him his lighter medication and told him where he was and what they believed had happened to him.

"You're in a hospital in San Pedro Sula. That's Honduras if you don't remember. You were found nearly dead in one of the most dangerous parts of the city. It's a hell on earth kind of place. The only reason any guy would go there was because he wanted a fix. We believe you got ripped off by the dealer and that you went alone because no one has called about a missing man. If you did go alone, the dealer likely decided to keep his drugs and take your money. We believe you put up a fight which explains your injuries. You received a concussion, several fractured ribs, a broken . . ."

Colin had stopped listening.

Colin Remembers

Katryna. Tryna.

Rocks tore open his jeans, they tore at his knees and knuckles, and blood mixed the dust to mud. His nose broke and ribs splintered as he was kicked and kicked and kicked. A boot pressed his head flat against the dirt road. He smelt the trash and shit worn into the ground and tasted iron.

"Arrástrolo aquí," a man spoke.

The voice was cruel and small. Colin could not see his the face of the man. Another man, a thoughtless goon, with a flat bulldog face covered in tattoos snarled and grabbed Colin's right foot and dragged him to the pitiless voice.
Colin kicked with his free left foot. It smashed into the man's nose and the man lost his grip.

"Mi nariz," the dog cried.

"Fair," Colin muttered and tried to stand.

The dog lunged at Colin.

"No lo toques, bastard," a woman screamed. It was anguish, both a plea for and warning for Colin's life.

The man with the small, cruel voice grabbed the woman. He wore a white sleeveless shirt. Like his dog, his face was covered in tattoos. His eyes were shaded black, cheeks were scarred, three letters inked his forehead. He threw her to the ground and spat, "Callate puta."

The woman quieted her cry and once more Colin was beaten. He was kicked until his body uncurled defenseless. Another tattooed man in a beater's shirt held his right arm down and a boot smashed the fist open on the stone street. Blood pooled in the cracks on the pavement and between the broken skin and bones of fingers.

Again, the cruel man spoke, "Recógelo."

A switchblade flicked against his throat as Colin was lifted to his feet.

"Mi nombre es Henry y eres un tonto Americano," spoke the man, "Esa es mi chica. La chica de Henry. Americano, crees que puedes tomar. Sin respeto. Te mostraré, podemos tomar lo que. Entonces los sabrás la próxima vez que preguntes."

'Sorry, I didn't see a tag on her," coughed Colin as someone drove a fist into his stomach. His breath lost as the fight was.

The woman was Katryna Maria Francisca Bengochea. Colin knew her as Tryna. They had met at a dirt floored bar two blocks from where a knife was held to his throat. The bar was for addicts and the forgotten. Men drank. Junkies snorted and shot. Few talked even the tweaked. Most of the noise came from a man in the corner. His face was worn with lines and his hands, tattooed with cobwebs, picked—open, one, three—on an out of tune guitar. Lazily, he slurred renditions of old songs.

Why you wanna take my life,
Why you wanna take the wife But it's so hard
It's so hard rollin' with no squad
You're like god, catchin' somethin' at the bar, the bar, the bar[16]

I'll never be able to escape that city, Colin thought as he stared at a shot glass after what he had hope would have blown away his thoughts.

---

[16] "It's So Hard" by Big Pun ft Donnell Jones. On *Yeeeah Baby*. New York City. Terror Squad Records and Loud Records. March 2000.

As he leaned forward, forearms square on the bar, steadying himself for the shot, a woman slid her right arm through his left, grabbed the shot and drank it. She kept her arm in his and she introduced herself with her full name and warned him she was dangerous. He let the tequila and cocaine work. He followed the lie Katryna offered and lost himself in her curves, her false smile and calloused hands.

He told her, "Toda mujer es."

She laughed and Colin signaled the barkeep for more shots. They drank. The smoked. They blew. They left.

That night, as thick copper curls fell and formed a canopy above his head and he ran his hands through her hair until his fingers stuck and he twisted his hands and pulled her head to his chest and she bit him and he did not release her head until his skin broke and blood stained her lips and she leaned back and the light of a streetlamp through the tattered curtain outlined her hourglass body, he let time slip and fell into the sheets, an avalanche.

I have begun to long for you
I who have no greed
I have begun to ask for you

With her, he forgot for a while. Then, as it always happened, when he was thankful to forget, he remembered.

The next week or three, they repeated that first night. Then, one night, as he walked with Katryna to get another drunk and another high, as he forgot and remembered, under the yellow glow of neon lights, in a back alley in a part of the world ignored, a place he should have never been, he found a knife pressed against his throat.

"*Antes de que tomaras algo de mí. Ahora tomaré lo mismo de ti,*" Henry told Colin and signaled to a man at the back of the group.

From the crowd, a man in whitewashed daisy dukes and a tube-top, striped golden and blue, appeared. As he walked towards Colin, he brushed his long curled and greased hair behind his right ear. Chancres pocked his forehead and jawline, and Colin held his breath as the man leaned in and whispered, "Soy Jimmy."

Colin could feel the oil from the man's hair as it fell against his face.

"Deberías haberme llevado a casa," continued Jimmy. "Entonces no habría habido violencia a menos que la quisieras."
Jimmy kissed Colin's cheek and cupped and squeezed between his legs.

Henry pulled the knife down and slit open Colin's shirt then tapped the knife on top of Jimmy's hand where it held Colin.

"Jimmy, darle algo para que nos recuerde."

"Henry, sabes que ningún hombre puede alejarse de mí sin nada."

Next a metal rod cracked against the base of Colin's skull and he toppled over. As he laid in the street, the dog walked to Katryna, twisted his hands through her copper hair, pulled, and dragged her away.

You say you've gone away from me
But I can feel when you breathe[17]

---

[17] "Avalanche" by Leonard Cohen. On *Songs of Love and Hate*. Columbia Records. 1971.

Rose Remembers

Colin looked back at Rose. Her hair was pulled back and she was wearing glasses.

"Do you remember something?" she asked.

"No. Not really. There's a girl, Tryna. Never mind."

"You do remember. Who is she?" Rose asked.

Her imagination ran and fear took over as she thought, *Oh dear God. His wife. His daughter. They took her, that's why he fought. It wasn't a robbery. It was ransom. That's why he won't talk. He is terrified.*

What she imagined before was better, it had put Colin at fault. Now she believed, or at least thought it possible, he was not whom she assumed. She saw Colin different. He had become a victim. She put down her notes and she looked at him. His eyes were clear, sedative free, the color glass takes when held in deep water. She saw past her chart for the first time and she felt his fear and pain. She wanted to soften those eyes because that was who she was. It was instinctive. Where she saw pain, she worked to stop it.

He desperately wanted help, yet he had become helpless and even more lost. He could not tell her his truth because he could not remember it. He had abandoned himself in his grief. He was without hope.

"She's nobody. She just . . . she's no one."

"What happened? Tell me, what do you remember?"

"I don't. Sorry." He picked up the small paper cup. "These the meds?"

Rose nodded. He swallowed the pills dry and he closed his eyes.

Uneasy, Rose left. *Why won't he talk? What won't he tell me?* she asked herself.

Then her thoughts turned to past horrors and the reasons why people did not or could not share what they knew. *Katryna, a woman, a girl. There was a girl, there is a girl. Has she been kidnapped? Where is she? I need to find her*, she thought and walked to her office.

That night Colin awoke terrified. He searched for a hope or a truth, he did not care which, that Katryna was alive. He prayed that she was not dead, that he had not gotten her killed. He found his truth in a lie. *They' wouldn't kill her and leave me,* he thought. *She'll get a scar somewhere, it'll be a reminder, but they won't kill her.*

Now

Colin watches as the water pools and whirls and drains at the bottom of the tub. Slowly he rolls his head under the water as it is spits, at random, from clogged rubber picks of the shower head. The pressure builds, releases, and builds again.

Oomycota, the Black Spores of the 47.

The water pulses and massages his shoulders and he tries to remember the last time he enjoyed a shower. He had paid the euro fee to join Rose at the gym the week before. But to stand in leisure with room to stretch is a comfort. He tries to argue away this small pleasure. *Why would I ever want this?* he thinks. *The last thing I need is clean. Clean's over. Shit's in. Haven't you heard, anarchy the new fad. It's returned like a fashion trend. Torn jeans and dirty nails. Fuck public works. Infrastructure be damned. We can swim in our shit filled rivers and drink beer cause it's the only clean water. Why wait for history to return to our roots, I don't have to die to live in the dirt.*

He smiles, the water won, and he is reminded of why these little acts are important to Rose.

To Rose, these showers, these rooms, these little bits of past normality remind her of the potential of tomorrow. She cannot resign her life to today as Colin has. These little breaks from cold nights, they keep her from becoming lost in his hopelessness. Rose becomes who she was in these little forty-eight hours of *playing house*. Colin knows this so he finds the money every time she asks, even if it's only for her.

He never argues with spending the money, although he does offer suggestions. The first time she stayed in a hostel after losing her apartment, Colin told her, "Never pay a rate where the charge is more than the number of beds. Find the spot with the seventeen euros for a bed in a room with eighteen others. What does it matter if you share a room with twelve strangers or twenty? Same bed, same shower. It's gonna be noisy and you're still gonna have to wait to piss."

Still, several times he gave her his last euro. Rose knew Colin cares for her, loves her as he can, and, at times, is in love with her; though, more importantly, she trusts him. Not with his words because he lies to himself but in his acts of faith towards her. He brings her food even when he does not eat. He puts his jacket on top her on the coldest nights. The only time she had seen him sober since *moving out* was when he gave her their last euros—43.70—to sleep inside for two nights at the start of winter.

BEFORE

ROSE

The morning after she slept inside and he slept somewhere else, Colin greeted her with coffee. His eyes were brighter than usual. They shined. The white lost the bloodshot hue and she saw the corneal scar in the lower left part of his left eye. His eyes clear, she fell in love with him again. *Maybe today,* she thought.

"Guy gave me a cup and told me to warm up," he said. "Told him I had a friend who was worse off so he bought a second cup."

He handed her the coffee. He gets a little more than most people because he always asked.

"It's easier to get two things from one guy than it is to get one thing from two since the first guy has already shown he's willing to give and finding someone willing to give is the hardest part," he drunkenly mused one night while drinking from a bottle some other drunk had given him.

Progress of a Parish Boy

She had seen him walk into a bar with four euros and leave it with twenty. They were always tourist bars and the bartenders helped him with his little charades.

One day for her own amusement she followed and watched the con.

She followed him to The Lucky, a four-leaf clover and Jameson paraphernalia kind of place in Trinity, the heart of Dublin's travel scene. A place that pumps Irish rock ballads on repeat. The High Kings, Dropkick Murphy, Van Morrison, Hozier blasted:

> *The only Heaven I'll be sent to*
> *Is when I'm alone with you*
> *I was born sick, but I love it*
> *Command me to be well*

Florescent lights lit the place bright enough to see one's reflection on the glossed bar. When he walked in, the bartender tilted his head towards a single guy who sat left of the taps in the middle of the bar. The cue told Colin the lone guest was waiting for friends. The bartender knew no wives and no girlfriends. Colin needed a group. As a rule, a group of friends traveled for the stories. The *do you remember when* conversations they would later laugh about. They wanted to try new things, visit weird places, and bond with some of the local strange. Couples traveled together, *to spend quality time together, to get away from it all*; and they did not want Colin taking away from that time.

Colin grabbed the seat next the guy and asked, "Ready for another?"

"Why not, it's Dublin right . . ."

Rose was too far away to hear the cliché de tourist-ism but figures she could fill in the blanks as she moved a bit closer.

A proper drinking city my gran always said . . .
Hell yes! I haven't remembered a holiday since '02. . .
I didn't come here for the weather . . .

Colin signaled for the bartender and ordered, "Two Beamishes."

Then he turned to the newcomer. "Trick of a drunk of this city. Beamish is practically Guinness but brewed down in Cork, you know, where they have the Blarney Stone. They don't like when you piss on it though, trust me you don't wanna be Joe Blank regardless of how much you wanna be like Tyler Durden. But Beamish, it's great and a few bucks cheaper."

"Nice. Thanks for the advice. Cheers!"

"Slainte!"
Rose vaguely listened to Colin talk the shite, but she did watch the guest as Colin spoke. He was absorbed.

"Beautiful City! Have you seen the Guinness factory?" Colin asked.

The guy shook his head.

"No! Amazing view. Plus, you've got to check out Kilmainham Gaol. Erie place. 'In the Name of the Father' with DDL and 'Michael Collins' with Liam Neeson were shot there. Check out Michael Collins if you haven't seen it. It's about the Irish Revolutionary at the turn of the 20th Century. He was actually shot, ya know, gun not camera, and killed down near where this beer you're drinking was made. About a mile north you'll find his grave. Beautiful grave. Set off to the side of Glasnevin Cemetery, knee high stone pillars and a large Calvary Cross the headstone, beautiful."

Shit...
Wow...
Nice...

Rose zoned out.

"You're American, how do you know all this?"

"I've made a few trips here before. Almost forgot, John Goodman made a movie there in the early 90s!"

"Where?"

"Kilmainham Goal."

"Sweet. I'll check it out with the guys later."

Colin turned and winked at her. The game was won. The friends of the tourist arrived and it was now the tourist's time to buy the round. Then it was his friend's turn, then the other friend's and the other. They bought and Colin talked himself into each round.

It was after the drinks, a few smokes borrowed, and stories told that Colin made the next day's rent for the bar stool at a regular haunt. With an ease as if he was with old friends, he confessed, "Bold of me but can anyone spot me a few euros? I don't have enough for cab fare and there isn't a bank close enough to rob."

Of course . . .
We got you . . .
Ten enough? Here's a twenty in case . . .

After the sixth or seventh round of drinks, Colin knows there is always someone who will help. Now with the twenty note in hand, tomorrow, he would avoid the mobs, sit and drink in quiet and listen to some old rock and roll as it played from a crap set of stereo speakers in someplace where he could take a swig from his flask as long as he bought beer.

With a simple thanks, he took his exit.

Amen, Amen, Amen
Take me to Church[18]

Colin never lied because there was no need. He just let people think what they would. That day, he was dirty, not yet filthy, but it was winter and everyone was dirty in winter. When people looked at his shoes they saw the salt and dirt from trashed filled snow, then they

---

[18] "Take me to Church," by Hozier. On *Hozier*. Rubyworks Records, Island Records, and Columbia Records. September 2013.

looked and saw theirs were only slightly more clean. Sure, their jackets had less dirt and their caps did not have holes, their gloves were not cut at the fingers and there was less dirt under their nails. But it was winter and everyone was dirty, so they did not need to bother themselves with why he happened to be a bit dirtier. They thought, *maybe, he is a painter . . . sculptor . . . musician . . . you know, he's a struggling artsy guy. He bought the first beer and, hey, at least he does not smell.* They lied to themselves because he was here and so were they. How could they explain themselves better without knowing more of who he was? And, since they did not want to know his truth, they did not ask. They kept their lives aligned with his so that they could sit next to him and explain Colin's differences in a way that did not hurt their conscious.

Also, Rose had never seen him beg. There seemed some code he walked by that got him drunk and buzzed without degrading others around him. Colin degraded himself. He gave up his life. He sold himself for a buzz and a smoke but he did not beg because that was not right, that was not true to self or lack of. A beggar reminded man of the faults in society and in the gaps where a man can slip into non-existence. A beggar was a premonition of the failure in man, a living ghost that haunted men for change, because the beggar, the man, a man did not make that choice. A beggar, a man forced to beg, was forced to because of societal structures he did not create. What was expected of one who begs? What was expected of a retired veteran whose resolve was lost in war, a child born with a mind that did not develop, a mother of four children whose spouse was dead, or an opioid addict? Did not all these men, these women, these children, confess the same? *I cannot help myself.* Did they not ask the same question, *Please, can you help me?* This appeal to emotion was the appeal to the heart in a broken part of humanity. These were the people imploring the world to help because the world was the reason they needed help. They did not start wars. They did not make tests. They did not set minimum wage. They did not choose their prescribed drugs. They were the mistakes in man so they appealed to men for help. They prayed to mankind and implored humanity to look at the face of its failure. Rose knew these men and women. Before from her work and now from her life.

Yet, the day she took the coffee, the extra one given to Colin, she was annoyed. She was glad Colin did not beg, for it allowed her to find that the faults in his life were his own and that allowed her to be angry and to challenge him. That day, however, he had done something he would have never done for himself; he had directly appealed to the emotions of a stranger. *I have a friend who is worse off.* She could hear the undertone plea of *help her*. She met him on his potential deathbed as he faced possible murder charges in a country known for having the worst hospitals and prisons in the world and she was worse off. He was drunk. Sure, he cared or, at least, tried to care for her, *to return the favor.* To her, he was like a record that skips. He was capable of being wonderful, full and passionate, he could be truly amazing, but then he would fall, he would skip, and his rhythm would be lost.

Help me! How dare he believed me worse off? she thought and, now, she was pissed. *Screw you, you martyr of self pity.*

She calmed herself and waited until that night, when his eyes were no longer clear, then she asked, "So you think I'm worse off?"

"Huh? What?"

"This morning you told the man with the coffees that I was worse off than you." Rose explained. "We're the same. Hell, at least I'm from Dublin and I'm waiting to hear from my appeal to the board. At least I have something. At least I haven't given up. What do you have?"

"I have nothing that's why you're worse off," he told her. He speech was slower and the booze made him annoyed enough to answer, to explain.

"Nothing is easy. I want nothing from today or tomorrow or yesterday other than to forget it. I watch people with indifference as they walk by. They could be wearing an Omega or a knockoff Fossil, driving an Audi or secondhand Fiat. They could be playing in the park with their kids, walking hand in hand with their lover, going on a run with their four-legged companion, or drinking tea with their partner of 50 years. What do I care? Why should I ever want what they have? I chose this life. I jumped in. You slipped and fell into it by accident. A girl who could not read the sign, 'Dead End,' because it was written in Latin and you skipped Latin class in high school to make out with Tom O'Mouthful."

"What are you talking about? I didn't . . .What?"

"You knew the rules. You broke the rules. You were caught. You were punished. Now you're angry about it. 'It's not fair!' you cried to them but why should they, the ominous they, care about poor little you? They don't and so here you are mad at me. You need your life to be better than mine because I have nothing. But I need nothing. Your wants, your hopes, your needs, are why you're worse off. Don't get pissed at me because you need life to be alright and you're terrified it won't be."

He extended his right arm from the middle of his chest with his palm up and mockingly waved his hand in a philosophic gesture. "I am here because I don't care what they or anyone does."

"Screw you," she told him and cried. "Yeah I don't want this but don't act like you do. Why don't you just fuck off!"

She was wrong and knew it. Colin did not want a thing other than a drunk that sent him to dreamless sleep or a high that passed the day without memory. Or, at least, he had buried those wants, those needs, too deep to find and now this was his truth. Most days even the booze and the drugs seemed more of habit than of need. It was just something he did. She was frightened and she was angry.

"Fuck off!" she repeated.

Without a word, Colin got up and left. That night, for the first time since before, she slept, fearful and alone, tucked away, hidden and forgotten, confused.

. . .

Confused, she was so confused.

She still could not believe it. Her job, *my life*, gone she thought as she packed up her apartment. The apartment was her home. She had grown here, cut into the door frame of the dining room was every inch of her life. Standing in the kitchen, she looked through a small window cut into the northern wall and down the hallway. Her childhood room was the second door on the right, across from it the bathroom. Directly ahead, at the end of the hall, was her parents' room, now her room, which opened to a small ensuite on the east and balcony on the west that connected to the living room. To her right, the west, was the door to the dining room and past that the living room. Besides the basics, chairs, sofas, tables, beds, and desks, all in their expected areas, the apartment was minimally decorated, souvenirs from her childhood and trips abroad were scattered across various surfaces and books filled empty shelves. They place had always looked as if she was in transit.

On a small, black and red portable record player, she lifted the needle, then walked to the balcony and lit one of her emergency cigarettes. She had smoked more these past months than in years.

Outside, Will Toledo's tight, southern voice was council. The Virginian wrote, then sung and arranged her thoughts.

> *In the backseat of my heart*
> *Our love tells me I'm a mess*

Below her was a small car park, beyond that Mountjoy Prison. As she sat there, on a small foldout chair, and took a drag from her cigarette, she remembered her father.

"It was right there, in oh, 1973, all hollows eves. Anyhow, it was right there Rosie," he would proclaim and point to the prison yard.

He was sitting on a stool in the corner of the balcony, next to the sliding door that led into the master bedroom. He wore an oversized wool sweater and loose jeans and slippers. As he told the story, he puffed at a short pipe. The light, warm smoke smelled of wood acorns and spiced rum.

"Your mom and I were sitting right here. It was midday, we were having tea, and a helicopter zoomed right by us. It was a small little guy, not meant for more than three or four people.

Well, it landed in the prison yard and all hell broke loose. Even over the noise, you could hear the guards yelling, 'Close the gates, close the fucking gates!'

It sure was a riot," he said and slapped his hands to his knees.

"Your mother and I believed the prisoners were trying to steal the helicopter, well, it turned out, they already had. A couple of IRA boys had hijacked the copter and were bustin' out a few of their buddies.

Oh, you should've seen the highlights."

Rose smiled then she looked up and saw The Mater Misericordiae University Hospital. It was where she had worked. It was where her mother had worked. It was where she had gone to school. It was why her father and mother had moved from Tullamore, a small town in the heart of Ireland, to the capital.

She pulled at her cigarettes, it was stale and tasted of wet twigs.

Her mother and father had bought the apartment after her mother had taken a job at the hospital. Built in 1861, on a small plot of land in Broadstone, a poor neighborhood two kilometers north of the

Liffey Bridge, the hospital now extended far beyond the original stone domus to the poor with modern wings of glass next the old limestone wards.

The hospital, Mater Misericordiae translated to Mother of Mercy, and this name, Rose felt shared the true purpose of the hospital. As a child, she had learned to love a place most feared. She remembered sitting in the bench, outside the trauma ward, as she waited for her mother after school. She learned that mercy, both towards self and others, was the only way to accept unbearable loss.

Then she had been fired.

Months ago, Rose had lost her job. She had taken one of the only vacations of her life and had gone to Berlin with her girlfriends. It was one last *girls only* weekend before her best friend got hitched so they partied. Dancing was never her thing but, with the help of a few friends, she found her rhythm. Molly and Snow White whitewashed the trip and she came back empty, her feelings checked and left at the gate in Berlin.

Two days later, she was given a surprise drug test, and she tested positive for MDA, cocaine, and a handful of illicit pills. A day after that her license to practice medicine was suspended, a month after, it was stripped, and she was escorted out of the hospital.

It had been several months since she had seen Colin yet since being fired, she often thought of him. She had started to understand his loss of self, through her own loss. Without her job, she could not be mad at him for risking it. *Hell, I wish he had been caught with my pills,* she thought as she pulled at her cigarette.

She could have explained the pills were stolen and been put on probation. Rightly, no one believed she did know she had taken the drugs.

Hell, I would've never taken drugs if on probation!

She finished the cigarette, then decided she would call around and leave a message at a few of his locals.

> *It's too late to articulate it*
> *That empty feeling*
> *You share the same fate as the people you hate*

She knew not to call but felt out of options. In other friends, Rose found support, she found sympathy. These friends were sorry for her loss and shared in her grief as they understood it. These were the friends that cried at her mother's then father's funeral, not for the loss of life, but for the pain Rose felt in the loss. These were the ones who wanted to help, and, because of them, Rose did not feel the depth of her grief for several months. These friends kept her distracted, they gave her a sense of purpose. Her life had been to give. She gave to her job, her patients, and her friends. Her job had fired her. She lost her patients, but her friends did not need her. Their lives were normal, simple, and beautiful. When she left home to travel the world, they had stayed and built homes with wives, husbands, children, and pets. Their jobs were stable and mortgages high, but controlled, and their vices were limited to coffee, TV dramas, pints of ice cream, and that third glass of wine. They were all pudgy and overworked but, overall, her friends were happy with the lives they had made.

They were the friends she wanted. They apologized and shifted some of the responsibility, some of the blame, to themselves; they personalized the acts and made themselves part of Rose's story. They tried to take some of Rose's pain, to share in her grief. But they were not the friends she needed; and, after a while, they became exhausted as they lived both their problems and hers. To them, Rose had lost her job, to Rose she had lost her life, and her friends could not relate to this because they had not. Their lives no longer synced, Rose and her grief became a burden because it was a grief they did not understand. They saw a job lost and told her *just* get another. They did not understand that in the loss of her job, Rose lost her purpose.

A few days later just before she was evicted, Colin showed. He was clean, well, in appearance. He had lost weight and his eyes, those blues eyes that stung when bright, were faded grey like a cloud covered sky lit by moon light.

Rose was so sad; she wanted her life back. She felt that he could, he would remind her of who she was.

"I'm sorry, I can't help," he told her.

Colin knew he could not share in Rose's pain because he barely lived with his own. Colin could offer nothing, and it was too easy to want nothing, when someone else shows that things are not needed. Colin was scared. Rose and he worked well when she was in control. In each other, they found escape from their separate lives. Rose could tinker, could fix, and Colin could forget. Their relationship was balanced through Rose's stability. To rely on Colin, Rose asked to become like him.

Blind in her pain, she asked him to stay.

> *Please listen to him*
> *It's not too late*
> *Turn off the engine*
> *Get out of the car*
> *And start to walk*[19]

---

[19] "Drunk Drivers/Killer Whales," Car Seat Headrest. On *Teens of Denial*. Matador Records. May 2016.

. . .

Colin had not left her alone, forgotten to the world, until she told him to *fuck off*. And, even then, when she woke in the morning, his jacket was laid on top her and he was asleep under an oak tree a few meters away.

Rose found that Colin never forced her to stay with him, he rarely even asked her to. He accepted her offers of kindness, as he had the coffee, and, as thanks for these kindnesses, he waited to repay them. As long as she needed him, believed to need him, Colin would never leave her. And when she asked him to, he would without a word.

Now

"What are you doing?" Rose screams at Colin when she realizes the sound from a second stream of water.

"I'm shaking hands with the President."

"Gross. Don't do that."

It is a habit of his she hates. He always pisses in the shower.
"It's sterile and I'm saving water. Gi would be proud."

"I don't know who Gi is but I'm not." She did not get half his references.

"Captain Planet: Earth, Wind, Water, Fire, Heart! Gi is the Asian chick who harnesses the Power of Water! Phil Collins' drum track. Classic."

"But seriously, if you let it rain down one more time, you'll come to fully understand Phil's wish."

"Terrible," he laughs and shakes his head. "Beer me."

"Your favorite," she says and tosses him a can. *He can be wonderful sometimes* she thinks and hopes she can keep this version of him for the night.

As the warm water runs down his chest and cold beer fills it, he smiles. Somethings from before can still make him smile now. The water has worn out the aches of weeks on the street. The beer fixes his want. He turns off the water and dries off in the tub. He tosses the empty can in the bin and Rose tosses him another. The toss is low. He drops the towel to make the catch. Fully exposed, he crouches over, can in hand. His hair is shaggy and his short beard outlines the side of his face. His jawline is taught, more from diet than exercise, and his skin is tight on his thin frame. He is skinny. *Too skinny,* she thinks then laughs.

"You look like young Golem with hair and without the ears! My precious!" she says and before he responds she is up and covers him with her hand.

"My precious," she repeats and takes him back to bed.

After they split both a beer and the döner in bed: grease, malts, and hops drip and mix with their sweat and stain the sheets.

BEFORE

ROSE

The day after Colin first spoke to her in Honduras, Rose returned to the hospital early to wait for a call back from the detectives investigating Colin's case. When she returned to her office, the day before, she had called every hospital and clinic and asked about a nondescript woman or girl with the name of Katryna. When the hospitals reported nothing, she called the police. They said they would check into it and call her back the next morning. She answered the phone at half past nine. The officer told her they knew of no ransom demands and that they did not believe the case involved a kidnapping. However, a dismembered body of a local woman was found east of the airport and another woman identified the remains as her daughter, Katryna Bengochea, from the crucifix, a family heirloom found on the body. Katryna was last seen by a friend with an unidentified man on Calle Principal two weeks before. The police told Rose that based on her story they believed Katryna was a witness to the robbery and killed for it.

They told Rose, "Do not talk to your patient, we need to get his statement. If you could, please prepare a private room."

Colin was rolled from the ICU into a surgical room. A theater window was framed to the left of the door and the operating table and instruments were pushed to the opposite wall. Old and crude equipment were scattered throughout the room. An eyelid clamp and sculptor's hammer with a set of steel chisels of various lengths were placed on the work stand and five bone saws hung from hooks to the left of a supply cabinet. The cabinet was out of place. It was homemade and painted white. It should have been in a kitchen filled with plates. Colin and his bed were pushed close to the far wall, left of the door. His back towards the window, he faced the medical equipment. A table was carried in and placed next to his bed and pinned him to the wall. Two cops, the two who always came, came in their dark suits and they were loud.

"No sé, no sé. Qué deberíamos preguntarle?"

"No sé, no sé. Qué debemos hacer?"

"No sé, no sé."

They laughed as they dragged metal chairs behind them. The first detective, the one who spoke with Rose that morning, tossed a pile of papers on the table. Facedown photos slid out and the date of the photos, five days past, was printed in a corner on each. A third man dressed more casually in a light blue, short-sleeve button down and khakis followed behind them. He did not make a sound.

"Sabemos que hablas español pero realizaremos esta entrevista a través de un traductor. No queremos ninguna confusión. Este homre va traducir o palabras exactamente para usted y luego sus palabras exactamente para nosotros," explained Cop 1.

"We know you speak Spanish but we're going to conduct this interview through a translator. We do not want any confusion. This man here is going to translate our words exactly to you then your words exactly to us," the silent man spoke, the silent man repeated.

"¿Cuál es tu nombre?"

"What is your name?"

"Que paso con Tryna?" Colin responded.

"Señor, por favor hable en inglés para que pueda se traducido."

'Sir, please speak in English so you can be translated."

"¿Cuál es tu nombre?"

"What is your name?"

"¿Que paso con Tryna?" Colin repeated.

The cops stared blankly at each other.

"What happened to Tryna?" Colin repeated, now furious.

The Cop 2 smiled at Cop 1. *He speaks* passed silently in the look between them. And without emotion, the silent man spoke, the silent man interpreted.

"¿Que paso con Tryna?"

"No conozco a Tryna. ¿Conoces a Tryna?"

"I do not know a Tryna. Do you know a Tryna?"

Cop 1 looked to Cop 2.

"No, no conozco a Tryna."

"No, I do not know a Tryna."

Cop 2 answered Cop 1.

"No conocemos a Tryna."

"We do not know a Tryna."

Cop 1 answered Colin.

"¿Cuál es tu nombre?"

"What is your name?"

Colin snapped.

"WHAT THE HELL! I wish I was your drugged out Chief! He'd have to be drugged out to make you two detectives! Then I could have the shit beat out of you and get two guys with brains in here!"

"¿Que paso Infierno? Desearía ser tu jefe drogado. Tendría que tomar drogas para hacerte detectives. Entonces podría sacarte un poquito de encima y conseguir dos tipos con cerebro aquí," automated the translator.

Colin was wrong. For the past days he had sat in silence and answered less to the cops' questions then they had his. They had tried. The doctors had tried. People wanted him to talk, they wanted to help but he had become a broken record on repeat with *I don't know* the answer to every question asked of him. Not even to the most pointless questions did he change his response. In his withdrawal, the cops and nurses and doctors played little games with him as they tried to reach the part of him that flashed in his eyes, as they waited for that perfect moment when the dope faded, yet his faculties were still split just enough, and he forgot his vow of silence.

"¿Qué debo comer, taco de carne o burrito de carne?"

"No sé."

"Do you think this tie matches?"

"I don't know."
"He oído hablar de esta revolución sexual en Estado Unidos. ¿Cual es tu preferencia?"

"I don't know."

"So a baby boy was born last night and they want to give it an American name. Any suggestions?"

"No sé."

When he woke up plastered in the hospital ward, he knew Katryna was dead and he knew Henry had killed her. He had felt her death like a night bite and, like the small death in the insect's prick, her death had lied dormant, a black spot that lived hidden deep in a part of himself no test could find. Before in his silence, he had let it hide, he had let it sleep; yet, now it had ruptured, it had spread, and Colin felt the death of Katryna and his exhaustion overcame his fear and he screamed.

"My name is Colin Lukends! I'm an American visiting Honduras. My passport is in a safe at a guesthouse in Felipe Zelaya. Now what happened to Katryna?"

He had not used his voice in weeks and rolled over coughing. His energy was spent, the fight was over, and he pathetically looked at the detectives, ashamed and terrified.

The translator took a soft and small breath and without inflection repeated:

"Mi llamo Colin Lukends. Soy un Americano visitando Honduras. Mi pasaporte está en una caja fuerte en una asa de huéspedes en Felipe Zelaya. ¿Y ahora qué le pasó a Tyrna?"

They had his attention because they had his answer. A detective flipped the pictures over and Colin inert, could lie no more. Katryna was dead.

The translator stood and quietly left the room and an officer spoke, "Señor Lukends, please tell us everything you know."

Now

Colin steps out of bed and walks to the window and opens the last can of beer. He stares out over the sprawl of the city, past where the old, limestone buildings melt into the blue-gold horizon, then down over the crawl of the street, through the people as they scurry home, eager to avoid the night. To Rose he looks a man at the edge of a boat in middle passage who eyes are fixed ahead yet looks at nothing. A man who knows not to look for land for he knows it too far, but instead looks into the variant hues of blue and looks to the shades for the answers men seek when the past is far behind and the future unseen. He carries the look of a man who wishes to fall and to have the tunnel, where the blue gives and the black takes, collapse around him.

Rose knows he will not stay long.

"Let's get a bite and a pint," he suggests as he collects his clothes.

"Colin, let's stay in. It's freezing. I'll grab a few more drinks before the shop closes. The döner wasn't half bad, I could do another with some . . ." she pauses just enough, "chips."

This is a silly jibe. Colin and she have been arguing over the entomology of The Fry for years. In a more jovial mood, Colin would stand from his stool and declare with a fry, the war banner, in hand:

"Heavily disputed is the origin of The Fry. The French, the Belgians, and the Spanish all lay claim to the advent of the French-ed cut potatoe fried in animal fat. For to fry them in anything else is sacrilege but that is another topic. The origin of The Fry does not matter but the name we call these slices of crispy golden deliciousness does. For we are no more than beasts if we lose the meaning in our words.

For hundreds of years the French have called these frites, the Dutch freiten, the Spanish fritas. In America the President was served a "French-ed potato" in 1802, and the most serious men, das Deutsch, have called them fritten since the 19th century.

But then, at the turn of the 20th century, in an attempt to change history and claim it for their own, as they too often do, the Brits declared, The Fry, a chip. They tried to claim, The Fry, a chip to make a thing their own. Heresy! Like that of the so called 'Glorious Revolution' when the Brits forced their beliefs on true believers. People of Ireland, men, women, and children, I ask that you call this evidence of God—for what is it not but perfect? And in God alone is a thing made perfect—by its rightful name and not by the name coined by the Brits. Do not let them steal something else from the world!"

Then he would order, "One lager and basket of fries please."

Tonight he only chuckles.

"Keep your chips. There's a cleverly named pub close by with a photo of JFK on the back wall, I'll get fries there. It's a short walk even in the cold. I'd rather not eat alone but I can't sit in this room. I'll walk you back after."

It is rare he asks her to join him. Colin knows Rose will not follow him and forget. He would never ask her to but he does not want to eat alone. If left alone, he will forfeit dinner to a heavier drunk and will eat only out of necessity; and, knows he will find this, a few bites and scraps from other men, with ease. Today, however, he wants to sit with Rose and eat with her, to share a meal, another, the last, fundamental act. They have drunk and had sex and have slept.

Eat. Drink. Sleep. Sex. Skip one at the cost of humanity.

These are intimate acts, they are the times a person is most vulnerable, when senses are lost in the bliss of a thing. When engaged in drink, eat, sleep, or sex, a person is not comfortable if alone. Before a person ate, drank, and slept in groups out of safety, fearful of the world. Now men eat, drink, and sleep in groups out of solidarity, of needing contact with the world. Monks who pray in silence, shut off from mankind, still come together to eat, drink, and sleep.

Sex by nature cannot be solitary and successful.
Again he looks out the window and down at Gardiner Street. Before, when he looked over an edge, he felt pulled, compelled by a nameless force to jump. Now he feels anxious, fearful of a push from an unseen hand. He is scared, he cannot eat alone, he cannot be left alone in his vulnerability. Without her, without Rose, he will drink alone and because of her, *her*, he will drink to forget he is.

"Fine," agrees Rose. "But I'm ordering dessert and wine even if the dessert is overpriced and the wine has been open for days. I know the bar. It was a favorite of Dad's after confession at St. Mary's on Saturdays. 'Gotta do something to report to the Big Man next week,' he'd say. 'If not, your mother would never let me leave the house.'"

Rose laughs at the memory. It is a sad laugh, a haunted laugh that through it passes love and pain. A pain that is defined by past love and love that is defined by former pain. Her love of her father cannot be understood without the pain of his death. In observation of his death, his life is remembered.

BEFORE

ROSE

"It's just time for me to go," her dad tried to explain.

"Why? Why do you need to?"

"I've already told you."

The room was laundered, sterile, and tasted of bleach. Rose always wondered why bleached tasted more than it smelled. The taste was like a soup, almost rancid, a day away from spoiling. At one point the smell of the soup, the taste of the soup was a comfort, was life. Then without thought, without discussion, it turned to poison.

How many memories I have of bleach, she thought as she sat next to her father.

From a small window beside the overused and uncomfortable lounge chair a little sun shone. The light was pathetic. The room was pathetic. It was not a comfort to rest, to die wedged between two cold, empty walls.

He doesn't deserve this! How dare they!

She knew this frustration, this anger. It was the anger of the hundreds she had tried to pacify. The multitude of frustrations, she had tried to explain away.

I'm sorry but this is the best we can do . . . NO! she screamed. *It can't be.*

Rose knew she could do not ask for more. There was nothing more to ask for. The past year, she had watched as her father quit. She could not understand why, *why*, he had given up.

Rose had fought death. She knew the war lost but some battles could be won. She was a knight but this night she dreaded and watched her father die.

Death, the old familiar Tuesday, made a Sunday.

To the right of the bed, an IV hung.

Drip . . . drip . . . drip, she watched her dad's life drop.

It's funny she thought, *drip, drip, drop, drop, it's not even blood.* The I.V., an hourglass, an executioner's countdown before the lever pull and the last drop.

Before, she had felt at a home in these rooms like it was the living room of her childhood where she used to study and play. Where everyone else felt trepidation, Rose had felt at peace. Even as her mother's figure wasted, her head bald from ineffective treatments, and the tumor spread, Rose was calm. Her mother's death was familiar. Rose understood it.

Cancer
A cell gone rogue
It sells and corrupts the rest

Now, Rose was lost. She was inconsolable. The expertise and awareness she brought, she gave to others, she could not understand for herself. Rose did not understand her father's death. *Why did he have to die!* Every test was negative. The doctors said he had quit that, in less than a year, his body had doubled in age.

Rose rested her father to the right of her mother in Tullamore, her parents' childhood home. It was a bright and clear day. The sky was azure along the horizon and cerulean at its crown. Grass, like chartreuse, grew along the foot paths and between the rows of headstones and pillars. The air was fresh, death did not linger.

This is wrong.

Rose wanted it to be raining, to be cold, to be grey, to be miserable. She wanted the world to feel like she did, but the world did not seem to care.

Their tombstones cut from a single granite slab, the shouldered, curtain tablets arched down and connected the two graves as a valley does two ridge lines that are part of the same chain. Carved into the headstones were a pair of Phoenixes and at the tympanums a Brigid's Cross. The woven, four armed cross carved into the stone, was the permanent ward against any future ill. Together, forever, they laid as they stood on their wedding day, side by side, and kept their vows even beyond death as they faced east, towards Dublin, towards the sunrise, and in wait of the rapture.

Rose always loved Tullamore, she believed it a fairytale city. It was the city were disasters turn to celebration. As she stood and looked down upon their graves, Rose could not escape the tales of her childhood.

This is wrong.

It was 1785," her father began, "when disaster crashed down upon Tullamore.

Early that year, a magician had come and he spoke of his travels. Of how he had travelled to the ends of the earth and how he had seen all the wonders of the land, but in all his travels he had seen nothing as wonderful as that which he had seen in the sky.

Then he asked, 'Who among you would like to come with me? Who would like to walk on the clouds and dance with the angles?'

Most were fearful. They believed this man a heretic. Only God had the power to raise men to heaven. Still, a few venturous souls, those whose father's father's were the legends of the times dared to join him.

So, up they went.

It was on the tenth of May, the magician and the daring men climbed aboard the transport to the sky and up, up, up they soared. Until, like Icarus, they dared too much, they flew too high, and with a boom they fell.
Below, the townsfolk fled as they watched a fireball from the sky come crashing down. Then they watched as the fireball spread and turned their town into ash.

Yet, the folk of Tullamore are hearty. The wind could not blow them away as it had the ashes. Instead they arose like a Phoenix, and they rebuilt, they resurrected the town."

She turned again to the top of the headstones and remembered the story. She remembered how it was here, at St. Joseph's Cemetery, in the heart of Ireland, halfway between Dublin to the east and the Cliffs of Moore to the west, on May 10 men and women came to celebrate and patiently wait for their resurrection.

Beside Rose stood her family, the family her parents had chosen, the family life had given them, Pete, Mags, Sam, Isle, Schmitt, and Patti. Behind them were a handful of friends and colleagues for moral support. The friends who tried to share in Rose's loss but would never understand it. The colleagues who did not save her father's life. And, behind them were a few distant relatives, who felt a need to say farewell to a man they did not know.

This is wrong.

When Rose returned to Dublin, she requested a leave of absence. The hospital had suggested two weeks, she suggested six months. Her father was her last little bit of home left in Dublin and she needed to break away from the city. Over the past two years, she had stayed in Dublin far too long and lost far too much. She needed to be anywhere else.

A week later, she was on a plane to a small underfunded hospital in the murder capital of the world.

Now

Rose smiles and wipes away a tear.

"You go," she tells him, "I'm gonna put on me face."

Colin bums a cigarette from some guy outside. He walks to the bar, Irish or American, and flicks his spent cigarette into a bin to the left of the dark, oak door. He pushes the heavy door open and takes the third seat in at the bar.

The bar top runs the length of the room with just enough room behind the twenty odd stools for a hefty man to squeeze by when he needs to visit the Jacks at the end of the room. Two round copper towers with four taps each are mounted at the center of the bar and black and white pictures and tin plates fill the walls. There are a few tables against the closed and dust covered bay window at the front of the room and, on each table, a white candle is stuck in an old whiskey bottle. Colin smells the day-old booze as the heat of the candles warms the air and fills the room. Yesterdays, old wax covered bottles are placed at the end of the bar. At the end of the bar, two regulars, drinking the regulars, sit in their regular seats. When a glass is nearly emptied the bartender fills up another with the same. Every other beer gets a whiskey back.

The bartender is old. He works meticulously and with a calm of experience. It is early and he is still setting up. Polishing wine glasses and hanging them above the bottles, he does not stop his work to greet Colin.

"Good'ay. What'll you have?"

"Pint of dark. Nothing fancy. I'll be puttin'em back."

"Easy enough."

He tosses a used coaster in front of Colin and fills a pint with a nutmeg lager.

"Gonna be three-fifty. Tab?"

Colin nods.

"Let me know when you're ready for the next one," the barman tells Colin and returns to polishing the stemware.
Colin lets the beer sit for a while and listens as Muses plays from a retrofitted jukebox in a back corner of the room.

> *It's plain to see it's trying to speak*
> *Cherished dreams forever asleep*[20]

He stares at the beer. The aching, penetrating vocals disorient. They strangle Colin. The song, it is obsessive, the tap of the drum, *bum, bum bum*, pulses and feeds a march into oblivion. He is scared. He feels a moment he too long feared is passing or has passed. He does not know. He sees the blood spots on the sleeve of his jacket and an image of Richard dead in the street. His hand feels as it did when it was broken in Honduras and he feels his panic as Katryna was dragged away. He takes back half the pint. He is choking, he is drowning. The water, the beer, fills his lungs.

His heart races, *bum, bum, bum.*

He finishes the pint. He . . .

"Thirsty, eh?" the old timer remarks and drops off another pint.

The voice breaks Colin's panic and he is pulled back.

---

[20] "Endlessly" by Muse. On *Absolution*. Westmeath, Ireland. London, England. Hollywood, USA. East West Records. Taste Records. 15 September 2003.

"Thanks. A whiskey and a glass of white as well."

The bartender pulls the dark bottle, topped with a Stelvin closure from the fridge. Colin knows it is an old bottle, the top twists off too easily and the tilt of the bottle too steep. At least, to make up for the taste, the pour is heavy. The whiskey is a yellow label, American bourbon with four red flowers.

He takes back the whiskey, the fire rages, his vision doubles.

At the front of the bar, the door opens and Rose walks in . . .

    Sarah walked in . . .

She is in blue jeans, dark boots and a brown wool coat. Her gold hair is up, tucked and tamed under a knitted red hat.

    She was in jeans, tan boat shoes, and an olive green peacoat. Her brown hair was down, the curls wild and free.

She takes, she took, off her jacket and lays, laid, it in on the back of the chair next to Colin.

BEFORE

COLIN

It was their first dinner together and their second date. The first date had been for lunch at Hemlock Falls, a small park in New Jersey. She drove. He took the train. They met during the day because they both secretly knew they could not meet at night. They were too busy with their separate lives in the mornings and days for a night to distract them. They picked up four lengua tacos from a food truck outside the park then they walked the trails and talked as they ate. The date was short. Colin does not remember much. He was nervous. She intimidated him, which confused him and made him more nervous. He fumbled over his feet and his words. He felt naked and exposed and pale from too many hours under florescent lights. Sarah saw in him the struggle of a confident man who was unsure. To Sarah, his faults were what made him real, made him approachable, and she loved him for them. By the end of their walk, Colin was so out of sorts, Sarah had to suggest a second date.

That night, their second date, they met in a bar in the West Village. It was small and intimate. A marble top, ten feet long and two feet deep, was the centerpiece. The backbar and stool tops were dark wood reclaimed from a barn in upstate New York; and, Edison bulbs caged in copper and black candles lit the room. The bartenders wore dark chambray button downs, slate wool bowties, and plaid aprons. Wine and whiskey were their specialties. It was why Colin had chosen this place. The small backbar was shelved with the whiskeys and in a cellar below was the wine. There was a hatch the bartenders used for the wines and a library ladder for the whiskeys. A daily drink special Two for One ran from Five to Nine. The bouncer outside controlled the crowd inside and the crowd inside kept to the rules.

- No Drunks. Keep Control of Yourself
- Be Kind. Keep Control of Your Mouth
- Men be Gentlemen. Take Off Your Hat and Let the Ladies Initiate
- This is a Bar. Drink or Go Elsewhere
- When Done. Pay and Leave, Do Not Linger Inside or Out
- Bartenders are Right. They are Always Right.

Salute Sasha

Colin got to the bar an hour early and gave the maitre'd twenty to let him save the bar stool. Then he tipped the bartender another twenty after the first drink. He watched the bartenders. He watched the crowd. It was mostly couples; they kept their eyes on each other and quietly talked. There were a few tourists, well, Colin guessed they were tourists. Their clothes, postures, and phrases were different, not bad, not better, just different. At the end of the bar, there were a few industry people on their day off. Colin knew they were restaurant workers by their nature. They were gruff. They drank heavy and watched everything then commented on everything in a coded language only those in the field really understood.

Colin sipped his second, now on the house, whiskey when Sarah walked in.

"Hey, you look . . ."

Colin started and stood. He did not know whether to shake her hand or kiss it, hug her or embrace her, kiss the air around her cheeks or kiss her. Their last date, their only other date, had ended as the first night they had met, with a small kissed on his cheek.

"Don't," said Sarah. "I've just put in days at the library."

" . . . I was going to say, real?"

"That's real-ly nice of you. Still, I appreciate the honesty." She winked and continued. "Anyways, sorry for the library pants, I got caught up and almost missed the train. I was reading this case, Bobbie Lee Brock vs Bobbie Lee Brock, heard of it?"

"I have not. Part of a case you're working or learning from, studying? I have no idea how our legal system works."

"Well, duh, that's how we wrote it so that us lawyers would always have a job." She teased. "But no, this has nothing to do with anything I'm working on. I stumbled across it while researching an entirely different topic. So, in 1995 a Virginian named Bobbie Lee Brock decided to sue Bobbie Lee Brock for five million dollars for violating his civil rights. His argument was that he violated his religious beliefs by getting drunk then 'going out and getting arrested.' But since he filed the suit as a ward of the state, he could not pay himself, therefore, he asked that Virginia pay."

"Clever."

"My thoughts exactly. Unfortunately, he lost. The judged ruled his claim 'totally ludicrous.' After, I naturally followed the White Rabbit into a world of ludicrous suits and became late." Sarah shrugged and continued. "Anyways, why here? Something great about this place?"

"No idea," Colin answered. "I figured if you didn't like it, you could chalk it up as the place and not my taste which gives me another opportunity to fail. But if you like it then of course it was my decision to come."

"Smart."

"Actually, I'm still working in a way."

"Never off the clock, are we?"

"Sort of. I'm developing an app from my fabled drinking habits."

"Oh, a legend in the NYC drinkers' circles, are you?"

"I am sorta a big deal. Not to brag but I do have the largest tab at my local haunt in Brooklyn. The owner told me not to worry about it and that when I've made my fortune, I'm to buy the building from him and charge him a dollar a month in rent. 'I give charity, I don't take it.' He tells me every time I try to pay."

"Well I should thank you then for sacrificing your Friday night to me."

"Not at all."

Colin was glad he came an hour early, he had found his nerves, and gained a bit of courage.

"The idea of the software," he continued, "is to allow users to create a customized 'bar crawl' of the city's food and beverage scene. It's basically from the countless emails and texts I've sent to friends that visited the city. Each one wants a different experience. How rich is their blood? What type of places do they like, dive bars, clubs, classic watering holes? What type of food? Etcetera. I would map out their night and send them on their way. The app is essentially the same. The user draw is that one spot along each crawl will have some sort of deal: a free drink, snack, or discounted door fee. We're here tonight because my buddy told me this is a good spot for happy hour drinks and snacks on the 'date night' crawl."

"Ah, okay, so I am an unknowing test subject. Well, now that I know this is for research, I suggest you save the receipts because the write off will be worth it." She turned to the bartender, "Dry white wine, something minerally and metallic, like I'm drinking quartz. Oh and your two favorite snacks. Surprise us, we'll eat anything, but it better go with the wine."

"Yes m'am," relied the bartender.

From the top corners of the room, music played, the voice, a soulful sprite, teased the room.

> *Hand down I'm too proud for love*
> *But with eyes shut, it's you I'm thinking of*

Like Sarah, it was playful and bright.
Sarah laughed then smiled that genuine smile that shared all her joy with those around her. Again, Colin fell in love with her. She was confident and self-aware, strong but gentle in her approach. When she said no, the rejected person was happy enough to have asked the question. Her acts innocently mischievous. If caught, she used that smile.

Later, as they left the bar, she pulled out a candelabra she had pocketed.

"No, I will not put this in my purse," she declared and glared at Colin.

Then turned and handed the candle stick to the bouncer. "Sorry about this," she explained. "I told him I liked it, so he took it. Boys in love, they'll do the dumbest things to impress you. Don't worry, I'll make sure he stays out of trouble."

She then laughed and smiled, that smile, and took Colin by the arm.

She already knew he would do anything to impress her. Silly as it was, had she asked for the candelabra, he would have taken it. He was scared of how she made him. Through all his shields and different masks, he was made. She undid him and found his true self.

> *I will never be the first to say it*
> *But still I do, you know I*
> *I would do it*
> *Push a button, pull the trigger, pull a mountain, jump off a cliff*

"Do you have the app?" she asked as they walked down the street.

"What?"

"Do you have your app? Does it work? Can we use it?"

"Sort of. It's not even in beta. It's really rough and only works in my neighborhood."

"Okay then Brooklyn here we come. I'll hail a cab and you can tell'em the address."

Seconds later, a green Prius pulled over.

South of Houston

"Crown Heights sir! This gentleman will let you know where," she told the driver.

"Brooklyn Bridge to Eastern Parkway. We're going somewhere between the Utica stops, I'll let you know a few blocks before."

"Okay, let me see this thing," she told Colin and took his phone. She clicked the small white square with a blurred and italicized S in gray on it. Onscreen the app opened.

Stumblr
Swipe left or right, it doesn't matter, you're drunk!

"Clever."

"I needed a name for the patent. Surprisingly, this one wasn't taken."

"Okay, let's play:

Type of Night:	*Date Night*
Hunger Level:	*Let's Eat*

Wine and snacks are done. I need a full meal.

  Cuisine Style: *Gastropub*

Yep. Grease and beers just what I need.

  Transportation: *Walking*
  Weather: *Warm and Clear*
  After Meal To Dos: *Desserts & Cocktails*
  Mood(s):   *Classy & Frisky*

Let us see. Bum. Bum. Bum. Loading, sorry, you think it would have been designed better," she teased.

"Okay, here we are. Driver, corner of Classon & Lincoln. We'll walk the rest of the way. Oh," she turned back to Colin and waved his phone. "I'm keeping this for the night. You're going to have to follow. I imagine this is going to be difficult for you, but I promise to not look at anything other than all of your photos and old messages with mom."

He hesitated.

"No need to argue. These are the two easiest ways to learn the quality of a man. Does he keep souvenirs of past lovers? And does he respect his mother? I don't have time to waste."

He did not care that she had his phone. There were times he let it die as he slept, to then wake up to two hours of peace before it charged. Although, he hated the wait when he turned it back on, the moments as the screen loaded made him antsy, as if the world had ended and he had missed the text. Still, those two hours of escape were worth a few seconds of anxiety. He knew Sarah would not find any texts with his mother. He had been raised by his grandmother after his mother and father had died in a car crash. It was something Sarah had not yet known. He very rarely spoke of them. He was three when they died and, when asked about them, he could only repeat the stories told to him by his grandparents. As for his text with his grandmother, she too was dead. Taken by old age at 94. Anyhow, she had used a landline with a spiral, off white elastic cable attached to a phone cradle until her death. And, as for souveniors, the only racy messages were from a high school buddy who found it hilarious to send pics of his genitalia. With one set, he had included the caption, "I'm getting a tattoo. What type of tree does this look like?" Next was the photo of the completed tattoo. He had decided on Maple.

Colin did care that he had no control and he did not surrender control easily. He was uncomfortable and disarmed when he did not know what was next. Even something as simple as not knowing their destination, a place he had been to before, made him uneasy.

Then Sarah, as if she knew his apprehension, looked at him, took his hand in hers, placed them in her lap, and shrugged as if to say, *So what if you don't know where you're going, I do, and you're with me.*

So he was and so he lets her take control.

They crossed the bridge and went down under it in a spell bound by an echo.

> *I think I'm a little bit, little bit*
> *Little bit in love you with*
> *But only if you're a little bit, little bit, little bit?*[21]

---

[21] "Little Bit," by Lykke Li. On *Youth Novels*. LL Records. September 2007.

Now

"I'll be right back and put your smile on, I should've warned you, you're not gonna get a quiet dinner," Rose says and walks towards the barkeep.

"Rosie!" hollers the old man behind the bar. "Well how are you my dear? It's been some time! Come and give an old man a squeeze."

The bartender walks out from behind the bar and gives Rose a hug.

"Hi, Uncle Pete. I'm doing alright. Takin' everything day by day. How's business?"

"About the same. Some days I can't pour fast enough and other days it's just me and the boys. You remember Sam and Schmitt. Boys get up off your ass for the first time today and give Rose a welcome. I know we don't see much of her since her folks've pasted but she's still family.

Sorry again about that. Tragic but can't say I don't understand. Suppose the lady upstairs goes to sing with the Big Man, I know I'd be soon to follow. Don't think I'd know how to pull my socks up without her."

She still did not understand.

"Why can't you stay?" she asked him far too many times. "Move in with me. A girl will always need her father."

And always, he answered, "My flower, you stopped needing me long ago. Just like me company that's all. Though, you know, I can't stay Rosie. I feel like a magnet being pulled. Your mother and I, we, ahh, she would've been fine. But me, I won't be right until I'm back with her."

"Thanks Pete. Now come here you two," Rose tells the two men as they stand from their stools. Sam and Schmitt are big, country boys from Balbriggan, a coastal town north of the city. Both are dockers and keep their family up north. They have come to Pete's for as long as they have worked the wharves.

"I see you've got your own chairs too."

Rose taps stools where copper plaques engraved with *Sam* or *Schmitt* are nailed to the backrest.

"Had to after Sam took a swing at some kid for not moving when told," tells Pete.

"This youngin'," explains Schmitt as he laughs, "Tells Sam, he'd been there for hours and, like a child, told Sam he didn't see his name written on it. So then Sam tells the kid, 'Yeah, well, I've been here for a few years more and you'd know this if you'd been here too.' Then knocks the kid right out off the stool."

Schmitt motions a punch towards Sam.

"Anyways, Rose, it's always a pleasure to see you beautiful," Schmitt tells Rose and gives her a hug. "The years might be tough but they don't seem to have beaten you down. You're as lovely as ever."

"Always the charmer Schmitt and, since I was taught to never lie, you look like a sacrificial cow! You've let yourself go. I can't believe Patti let this happen," Rose laughs and taps Schmitt's stomach a few times with the back of her hand.

"This is the look of a man who no longer runs for nickels but uses a pen to write the big bucks."

"Gaff," Rose replies and smiles. It is a smile free from the station of her life and, again, for the second time today, Colin notices how beautiful she is.

"How about you Sam?" Rose asks. "You look, well, the same. You two look like you've spent every part of your life outside marriage bed together."

"Desk job like Schmitt." Sam answers and likewise hugs Rose. "Better pay, bigger stomach. The kids are fine. First is about to go off to Uni down in Köln. Tells me he's gonna design the ships I've been staring at for decades. Schmitt's got some family down there and they're gonna put him up until he finds a place."

"Wonderful. Speaking of half brained fully cocked Irishman off in the world, how is your brother out in San Fransico." Rose asks Pete.

"You know, says he's gonna come back for a visit then says he's too busy. Says he's gonna sell his pub, then says he's not. Guess I'd have to drop the 'American' part if he ever does. Though if I'm lucky, I'll beat him to retirement."

"Glad to hear you two are keeping the rivalry going."

Rose then turns and motions to Colin who finally stands from the bar and joins the welcome party.

"Well guys," she continues, "this is a friend of mine, Colin. Met him out in Honduras, he's an American so be nice. We all know how sensitive they are."

"Pete, Sam, Schmitt. Rose mentioned she knew the place but she didn't clue me in that she knew the faces as well. Glad to meet you. And Uncle? I'm shocked. Cheers!"

Colin lifts and finishes the pint. Pete fills him another.

"Close friend of the family is all," explains Pete. "I went to school with her mum and dad. Sam and Schmitt are tenants of about 20 years."

"Met Rose after her First Communion," tells Schmitt. "Pete offered his place for the reception. It was the miracle of the booze never ended. I remember Father Daughtry was so deep, he blessed a few bottles, asked if there were Protestants present, then baptized'em in the name of the malted spirits. Ahh what a day. You remember Sam? You picked up Isle, tossed her over your shoulder and cried, 'We'll be back shortly, I just wanna make sure we can have another party like this in a couple of years.' Isle grabbed a bottle of wine and cracked you for it."

"Eh still got the scar." Sam pulls back his hair and shows a quarter sized bald spot behind his left ear. "Worst part. We actually had Ian nine months later."

"Colin, Rose, take the two seats at the end far end of the bar, next to Sam and Schmitt," Pete tells them and walks back behind the bar. "I'm gonna go tell Mags you're here. Know she'll want to say hello and cook up something good. Steak good? Wait, finished that yesterday. We got in a few chickens earlier. I'm gonna tell Mags to roast a few birds. Sam and Schmitt, you're in luck today, I'll be putting food in your mouth at the cost of mine."

Pete refills their drinks, opening a new bottle of white for Rose then pours five whiskeys.

"I see you're still pouring dad's favorite," remarks Rose. It is Four Roses: Yellow Label.

"He had good taste," Pete replies and winks at Rose. "Slainte."

Pete takes his shot then shouts into the kitchen and walks up the stairs that run behind the back bar. The bottles lightly shake with each step.

A young guy in skinny jeans, an over-sized shirt and fitted hat worn backwards, slides past Colin and walks past the rest of the group. He smells of smoke and sex. He glances back towards the group as he walks into the restroom.

The dinner and company take away the past. The present comes and Colin and Rose forget. Colin is charming, Rose is reminded why she loves him. She wants him to be the man of tonight. He is in control. He is stable and confident as if the world is his. Even when asked how they met, he laughs.

"Okay I was down in Honduras. It was one of those trips, the kind you keep between you and the buddy that goes. We go down and, you know, its Honduras. Tequila. Señoritas. A little bit more."

Again, the young guy with oversized shirt walks past. This time to the jukebox. He puts in a five note and enters his song codes. Justin Timberlake plays.

> *Keeps coming closer*
> *I don't but she thinks I know her*
> *Beautiful smile with those sad eyes*

Colin glances at the guy then turns back to the conversation.

"Short story, I met Rose because my buddy gets ousted from a hotel.

Long story, my buddy and I take a trip to Honduras. We're taking a week away from it all. As you do in these situations, I find myself at the hotel pool with an absolutely wonderful woman. Ladies, please, don't judge me for this next part. So I'm at the pool and the next thing I know my buddy is screaming my name, 'Colin. Colin. Shit! Colin.' He is naked and holding a pillow over his, well, you get me.

'She's dead. Fuck dude. She's dead.' He's completely loaded, I mean, you can see the white under his nose as he screams this across the pool.

I'm at a complete loss. Security is chasing him down. 'Sir, Sir, Sir, you have to calm down. Señor. Stop. Come with us. Señor, Señor, Señor, stop. Please stop. Por vavor! Let's put some clothes on and tell us what happened. Sir, please.'

I swear to you. Next thing, he's surrounded, so he jumps in the pool and starts swimming towards me to avoid the guards. He gets out, and, of course, the guards are right there—the pool was tiny—anyways, they wrap him in a towel, I settle him down, and we go back with security to the room. There is blood everywhere and his room is raided. Clothes, money, drugs, everything of value is gone. The woman is gone and he is too tweaked out to tell us what happened. Security tells him to put on some clothes, so I give him some of mine, and we all take a walk to their office.

Finally he settles down enough to tell us what is happening.

Apparently my buddy and a woman were going at it in the shower. To better position themselves they stepped out of the shower to use the toilet for balance. Then my buddy decided he wanted to take a line off this woman but he didn't want to stop in order to get it. So, he picked her up and swung around and her head cracked against the edge of the sink. He looked down, saw a lifeless body on the floor, a ton of blood, and freaked. Next he dropped her and ran through the hotel screaming my name. Along the way, he picked up the pillow from a couch in the hallway.

Now we were terrified. Did he kill her? If so, where did the body go? Naturally, we checked the cameras, and the footage showed her leaving the room five minutes after holding his travel bag and a towel to her head. She used a service exit and, since security was too busy trying to catch a naked, cracked out gringo running through the hotel screaming, 'She's dead!' nobody noticed her.

So, obviously, he gets kicked out and we find another hotel in a shadier part of town. Then, conveniently, he gets a call from work and has to go back to the States two days early. I think, 'Hell I'll be safer without him.' Apparently not. One of those two nights left, I drank a bit too much tequila at the hotel then I followed guys in suits to an even shadier part of town where we drank even more tequila. I left and I hailed a cab and fell asleep in said cab. When I came to, I was at an ATM being forced to take out the max. I was being robbed and the tequila didn't like that because without money there would no longer be tequila. I took a beating. Stupid me, money wasn't worth the risk but at the time I wasn't thinking. I met Rose the next morning and she put me back together."

Colin takes Rose's hand, squeezes it, and kisses her cheek.

Rose knew the story. It is not Colin's but the story of another patient in the ICU. She did not care he lied. She did not care they, Pete, Mags, Sam, and Schmitt, knew the story a lie. Tonight, when she did not live her own truth, how could she ask him to. Tonight, she is between jobs and wanting to do something new whenever asked about work. Tonight, she is living close to Phoenix Park because she wanted a place with a view.

> *I almost forgot*
> *Who are you*
> *I try to forget every time I see ya*

After dinner, Colin steps outside for a smoke. The young guy from the jukebox is leaning against the wall under a neon sign.
"Boge?" Colin asks the kid.

The kid hands Colin a cigarette and a light.

"Thanks."

"You're Colin right? Jonny's buddy from the Lizard?" the kid asks. "I've seen you in there a few times. Saw you talking with Dickie last night. You know anything about what happened?"

Again, Colin sees Richard dead in the alley, Katryna pulled away screaming, and Sarah in her wedding dress.

> *This is turning into some type of amnesia*
> *I need ya*
> *Memories fade away*[22]

---

[22] "Amnesia," by Justin Timberlake. On *The 20/20 Experience—2 of 2*. RCA Records September 2013.

Before

Colin

Colin worked. Sarah studied. They saw each other on weekends. He had moved out of the crowded Crown Heights apartment and into a studio in Chinatown. The smell of salt and fish, his morning coffee.

It was Sarah's last semester and three years since they met. His app had officially launched six months before. A restaurant group liked the idea and invested. It now had 225 full time employees across the US and each employee designed customs tours of a city's nightlife. In addition, they had hired teams of part time workers to pound the pavement and promote the service. Since it launched, three million people had used the service. Colin was busy. Still, each weekend Sarah and he tested a crawl like they had that first night. At some point, Colin had stopped working for his idea and started working for her. He built those nights, he made those plans, for her. His world became the world he wanted to have with her. Those nights they walked and they ate and drank and laughed and loved. Sure, he planned those nights, but she controlled them and took them anywhere else she liked.

He asked her to marry him the day she passed the Bar Exam. He met her outside the test center. He knew she would pass. He asked her to open Stumblr and to choose the crawl from that spot. There was only one option. He had designed this crawl for the occasion and locked it specifically to his account. The last thing he wanted was for some new user to click it then unknowingly propose.

He gave her a dozen blue and white lilies. She preferred lilies to roses.

"I get it. Roses have thorns and must be picked and held softly, yadda yadda yadda, one must be careful with roses as one is with love. But I prefer lilies." She had told him the first and only time he had brought her roses.

Lilies in hand, he led her to a white '65 Mustang convertible, top down. A buddy in a chauffeur's cap and tacky tuxedo t-shirt exited the car then opened the passenger side door and folded down the front seat. Sarah stepped in and Colin followed.

First stop, Hemlock Falls, they walked and ate beef tongue tacos.

Colin wore the same outfit he wore the night he met her. Black Wingtip Oxfords, dark gray slacks, and a white button down.
Sarah wore her comfy study clothes, dark spandex and a light sweatshirt. Her hair was pulled back and lines from her reading glasses marked her face.

"You should've let me change," she told him. "Feel a little under dressed. Especially since, well, I know what you're doing."

She winked and he fell into the comfort of knowing she was in control.

"Your bag is in the car. We'll go to the hotel after."

Then he winked and she laughed. They walked the trail and ate in silence. The small, intimate glances they shared passed more than any words could. They both knew the promises made in that walk.

At a small bridge, her phone buzzed and *You're Here* flashed on the screen and "Made to Love" by John Legend played softly.

> *Oh have you ever known*
> *When you laid your eyes on*
> *The perfect work of art*

I knew right from the start[23]

Again, like the first time they walked this park, Colin stumbled over his words.

"I don't remember much of the last time we were here. You scared me. You saw me. But I know that I can never be lost with you because you will always know where we're going. I love you. Marry Me?"

"Of course," she replied and kissed him.

After, they went to the Plaza. The lobby, the elevator, the rooms, were classic and iconic New York City. In a city that was always moving, always building, this old hotel felt tacky, out of place. It was gaudy. The lobby was spacious, almost cavernous with no natural light. The chandeliers lit the room and the light bounced off the marble and bronze and gold. The elevator had a bellhop who wore that small, can cap. He slid the metal cage, painted in gold, open and ushered their way inside. The room was on the tenth floor. It was basic: bed, bath, and desk. The money spent was for the view. The windows faced north, below was the hustle of W 59th Street, and just on the other side Central Park sprawled out before them. The buildings on the far side were dwarfed. It was one of the few places one could stand at a window and not feel the eyes of others looking back. It transported them. The city was no longer home, they were away, they had escaped. It was a fantasy. They ordered room service, a bottle of bubbles, then played in the sheets for a while. After, they wandered Central Park and ate overpriced hot dogs and listened to a street performer cover George Harrison.

> *What is life without your life*
> *Tell me, who am I without you, by my side?*[24]

---

[23] "Made to Love," by John Legend. On *Love in the Future*. Good Records and Columbia Records. August 2013.

[24] "What is Life," by George Harrison. On *All Things Must Pass*. Side Two. Apple Records. February 1971.

Then, before they had decided on a date, a venue, those to invite, Sarah died. A month after the proposal, she had begun to complain of headaches and was often nauseous. When she went to a hospital, she was diagnosed with an aggressive brain tumor. She was told she had less than 15 months to live.

Globlastoma. Harrison again, same set just the other side . . .

> *Mind can blow those clouds away*
> *And all things must pass*[25]

"I guess planning my wedding will be the death of me," she joked.

She smiled and he cried. Both were confused and terrified and hurt by a loss that had yet to happen. Sarah was sitting in front of him telling him she was going to die and he felt the grief and pain as if she had already passed.

Colin took a leave of absence as CEO and they took a trip. They used the money for the wedding and they visited cities where Stumblr had launched. The trip was a blur. A week in Tokyo for ramen and sake, another in Paris for poetry and absinthe, then Edinburgh for Scotch and Ceilidhs, Berlin for anarchists and artists, and Barcelona for wine and Dahli. They went to Miami for rum and pork and New Orleans for jazz and rum and gin and whiskey and vodka, Austin for whiskey, Phoenix for tacos, San Diego for beer, San Francisco for late eats, Seattle for doughnuts, Montreal for bagels and poutine, and Boston for history and seafood.

It was a dream, a grayscale of raw emotion.

She had told him if he cried before they got back, she would board the first flight home. "I still alive,
don't remind me I won't be."

---

[25] "All Things Must Pass," by George Harrison. On *All Things Must Pass*. Side Three. Apple Records. February 1971.

She had said this for him, Sarah wanted to remind Colin of the reasons to live. She felt his pain because she felt her loss through him, it was through his suffering that she felt the impact of her own death, and she wanted him to find and remember the joy of their time together, not the suffering of their time apart. Still, behind every smile of the trip, there were tears. In the day, they delved in one another, in their love; but at night, when she slept, and with sleep too familiar to death, he wandered as he tried to escape the pain and keep true to her request. She would never see him cry so he walked the nights and lived out his nightmare.

Before, before he knew she was dead, the crawls were spontaneous. He, she, they, looked forward to the next place as much as the current one. Before, they looked at a piece of art or tried a new cheese or chocolate in comfort of the present and in wonder, in fervor of the next. Now he just wanted to stop, to pause, to never move on. He wanted to stop moving forward and stay forever in that one place, any place, because a new place was closer to the end, her end, their end. As the trip ended, as their lives together ended, as each new place became the last place, he could not remember anything other than her last, their final, stop was even closer. The trip became the time of their life and the time left in it. It was a countdown.

He just wanted to stop and find a moment and become trapped in it with her.

Colin married Sarah a week before she was buried. They used the get-well bouquets as their arrangements; red, blue, yellow, and green pansies, daisies, and carnations spotted the room.

"Color scheme be damned!" Sarah declared.

The little hair she had, she kept in a loose braid on the right to hide the scar. Her wedding dress was the egg shell hospital robe.

"Picked it out myself," she told him and laughed.

When Jane called her Princess, she asked if the Force could cure cancer.

Colin sat next to Sarah in chair, faded and worn from the hours of wear, and wore a white button down and black bow tie with white polka dots. They held hands and an I.V. drip kept rhythm as they spoke their vows. And true to their love, they spoke their vows in the present. They were grateful for each second and, in those seconds, as they looked at each other and spoke, they forgot the sorrows of the future and remembered the joys of the past and cherished the moment.

She chuckled and put a cloth to her mouth and coughed as she said, "Don't know why we're doing this anyways, you know this will never be ex officio."

Colin knew there was a joke and smiled under watered eyes.

"It won't be consummated," she added. "And, honestly, who would ever want that. It takes the whole reason out of getting married."

Sarah ended hers vows with, "I, Sarah Reznick, will love you forever. But you must love again. Do not let my memory haunt you. Do not hide from the world. I will marry you today, but you must love another. My dying wish is for someone else to know the love that I have."

Then as it did the day Colin asked Sarah to spend what would be the rest of her life with him, John Legend's *Made to Love* played.

> *I was never sure of a God before*
> *But I knew he must exist*
> *He created this*
> *I was made to love*

They rocked slowly back and forth, hands clutched between their chests.

It was their only dance. As Colin looked into her color faded eyes and he saw death, he knew the lie as he spoke it. He promised her he would love again but he would not, not like this. He would never be able to give this love to another because Colin had not given his love to Sarah, she had taken it, so with her death, it went.

> *You were sent for me too*
> *I was made to love*[26]

Colin did not go to the funeral. Her funeral was for her family and friends. It was not for him. She was his and he was hers. It is a mystery of faith that man and woman become one flesh. It is not a mystery that he did not need to say goodbye. He knew she was gone. It was absolute for him. For it was loss of self and he could not escape this loss. Her life, their life, had become a myth. Everything was haunted. He could not escape her, because in her, he define everything.

A day after she passed, he made breakfast in their apartment and for hours he laughed and cried in mania, in his boxers and socks on the cold, faux wood floor, clutching a yellow and blue silicon spatula that read, *Someone got laid*. She had bought it for him as a housewarming gift.

She's everywhere.

For an entire night, he sat on the couch and stared at a drywall patch behind the TV and took swigs from a bottle of whiskey. Sarah had sworn she heard a rat in the wall, so he opened it up and laid a few traps. After a month without a single kill, he patched the hole.

She's everywhere.

---

[26] "Made to Love," by John Legend. On *Love in the Future*. Good Records and Columbia Records. August 2013.

After the bottle, he hugged the toilet bowl. Tears fell and splashed and mixed with bile. He cleaned himself up with holiday hand towels. She had picked out the towels.

She's everywhere.

Before Sarah was alive and Colin felt she had passed. Now she was dead and he could not escape her. He had turned her into a possession because he had turned her into everything. He had made her eternal and inescapable. He had made her into a creation and in this myth had lost his reality. Fated, his future rapt in a soft, honeyed contralto.

> *If you build yourself a myth*
> *You'd know just what to give*
> *What comes after this*
> *Momentary Bliss*
> *Consequence of what you do to me*[27]

He had to leave.

He paid a two month advance on his rent and told his landlord to find a new tenant. Then he packed a black duffel bag, and sent a text to Isaac, *I'm gotta get away for a while. Take anything you want from the apartment. I won't be back before it's gutted.*

He called his company's attorney and told him to draft and sign his resignation letter. He grabbed his passport, ignored his phone and keys on the side table next to the door, and left.

---

[27] "Myth," by Beach House. On *Bloom*. Sub Pop Records and Bella Union Records. March 2012.

Now

Again, the teen asks Colin under the neon light of the Irish or American, "You know anything about what happened?"

"Sorry," answers Colin and he took a drag of his cigarette. "Dickie, don't know him. Why what happened?"

"Dickie, the balding Queen Victoria size Boss Godfrey."

Colin shakes his head.

"The fat man with aviators and out of date leather jacket. He bought you drinks last night. Kyi saw you with him."

"Kyi?"

"A skinny twink with blacked out goggles at the bar yesterday. I know you don't know him. He got your name from Jonny."

Colin thinks and takes a drag from his cigarette.

"Richard bought me drink, yea. We stepped outside for a smoke. Told him thanks and left. He followed for a bit, angry that I wasn't properly showing my thanks for his hospitality." Colin shrugs. "He walked slow, I don't. No idea where he went."

"That's, that's the thing. He didn't make it anywhere. Somebody killed him a few blocks from his place. Cops are holding anyone that might've known something. Assholes shut down the Lizard and took Jonny in. They figure it had to be one of his old busts, you know, pissed off, looking for revenge. I mean, I don't like cops, I've had my problems with a few, but Dickie, sure, he was an old horny bastard, but he was a good one."

"Wait, Richard was a cop?"

"Yea, well, he had retired but why else would he dress like that."

The kid tosses his cigarette in a bin. "Look, I don't think anyone is gonna tell the cops you were with him. Just wanted you to know since you're friends with Pete and Mags and they're good people. So that's the craic."

The guy turns and unlocks a stairwell door to the right of the bar. He walks up the stairs and a light on the third floor comes on. Colin pulls at his cigarette and forces his lungs to hold and absorb the smoke. Then he tosses his cigarette and steps back into the bar.

At the table, Rose asks what is wrong. He is shaky and his breath is shallow. Colin ignores the question and asks Pete for the bottle of whiskey then pours himself a tall glass and takes it in one go.

"Sorry," he tells the group. "I had a strange conversation with the guy on the third floor. You know the kid walking up and down the bar earlier?"

"Kyi? Nice kid, bit off, but pays his bills and never give us any trouble," Pete responds.

"He's Kyi?"

"Yeah, does the whole third person bit. Guessin' he did that. What'd he say?"

"Nothing really, sorry, just some stuff he said brought up a few memories I wanted to forget."

"Well, we all have some of those, don't we!" Schmitt laughs and looks to Sam.

Sam shakes his head.

"You know, Sam and I weren't always the responsible ones you see today," explains Schmitt in an attempt to restart the party. "One time, we were real hungover and in need of a few extra Z's. So, we hatched an ingenious plan. We strapped together two straw man, well, we used carton paper, but anyhow, and set them up on the docks so their shadows could be seen by the bosses. Then we passed out in one of the cargo bins. Woke up to it being loaded onto a ship heading, damn can't remember, but it was far."

"South Korea," interrupts Sam. "We were on a boat that was going to South Korea."

"Ahh, that's right," laughs Schmitt. "Good booze I hear that way, would've been one wild story."

"So, Schmitt what happened?" asked Rose.

"What do you mean?"

"What happened after you woke up?"

"Well, that part is boring. We got off the boat and got caught. Our visionary scheme was discovered. Apparently, a gust of wind literally blew it away, so the responsible ones of the time gave us a long talk and we worked night shifts for three months."

"Yep and I got it again when I got home," Sam adds. "Isle was not happy about the night shifts. Charlotte, our second, was four months at the time. And, on that blissful memory, if I don't wanna have a repeat of that conversation, I need to get going. Three days off from being the boss, which means it's back to taking orders. Mag's thank you for dinner. Pete, you as well. Schmitt talk tomorrow."

Sam stands and gives Rose a hug.

"If you need anything, you ask," he tells Rose. "Good meeting you Colin, take care of our girl here."

Sam and Colin shake hands and Sam takes his leave.

Rose looks at Colin. She knows he too wants to leave though she is scared. She knows that when they do, he will. He will walk her back to their room, but he will not stay. She wants him to stay, to talk to her, but knows she cannot ask. He will only admit his truths when blind drunk. It is sad that he is truthful about himself and to himself only when he no longer is himself, when the booze takes control, confessions flow.

Rose does not want to leave him, but she will not follow him, hoping for an admission he will forget he told. At night his depression folds over him. In the day, he is a companion of sorts. Pain is felt and shared. Laughs are exchanged. Hands are held. At night, he is gone. When she walks with him, she is reminded of the soft and sad cries at the hospital that were just loud enough to keep the other patients awake and, eventually, always someone would scream in frustration and exhaustion at those cries.

When she walks with him, she wants scream.

Colin wants to hide. He wants obscurity.

Why did I have to go to the Lizard? he asks himself, he blames himself.

There are hundreds of bars in Dublin and he could drink at nearly all of them without being known but he does not go to those bars. He frequents the same bars and he lies to himself that it is the cheap drinks that keep him going. The truth is that these people at these bars accept him and he needs the acceptance. They do not ask him questions, they let him drink in peace, in quiet, in the comfort of people that know him or know enough of him to leave him alone. These are the places he has gotten too drunk and talked about his past. Some people even listened. Even this want of obscurity is a lie. He wants to stop feeling and he cannot so he pretends and hopes that isolation is close enough. But at night, like the last nights with Sarah, he cannot pretend, so he goes to the places that have accepted him for this lie. Sadly, he cannot share this with Rose because Rose reminds Colin to be who he was before, to be the man that Sarah loved, to be the man that made her a promise, a vow, but to be that man, he has to admit and accept her loss and his pain, which he cannot do.

Rose accepts Colin's need to leave.

"I think we should get going too. Tonight has been wonderful. Thank you, Uncle Pete and Auntie Mags," Rose says and stands. She taps Schmitt on the stomach, smiles at the big man and adds, "Watch the weight."

Colin leaves and Rose follows.

Before she can walk out, Pete grabs her arm and pulls her close for a last hug.

"I'm glad you walked in tonight," Pete tells her. "I've heard some rumors, no need to talk about'em. But I'm getting old and tired and I need someone I trust to help me out around here. Before you say anything, don't. Go try and fix what you need, that man there's holding a lot of weight, and I know you wanna take some of it. You're too much like your mother, bless her, now go and come back soon. Love you Rosie."

"Thank you Uncle Pete."

Rose leaves to find Colin.

BEFORE

COLIN

Colin had to leave and, on the fourth day after she died, he did.

He stepped down as CEO. The company had grown with, had grown from, his relationship with Sarah and she was dead. The faces, the walls, the logos, they were the traits of a child that resembled the mother. He could not think of work and not think of her. He had to bury it with her.

He took the A-train to Howard Beach towards Far Rockaway then took the Airtrain to Terminal 4 at JFK. The trip was menial unlike the first trip, years ago, when he took his first flight out of JFK, and was full of worry: worry that he missed his stop, worry that he bought the wrong ticket, worry that he went to the wrong terminal, worry that he missed his flight . . . He did not remember that trip and he did not care about this one. This trip did not have a purpose. Nowhere was its destination. Any and all was the time of departure.

Inside, the terminal was spacious, glossy, and industrial. He passed under the overhead board with departure/arrival times. He stopped, took a glance back at the board, *Fuck it*, he thought and got in line. He hated lines. When he wanted to get somewhere, he hated delays. He could have bought the ticket with a single click on his phone but he had left his phone on the table in his, in their, apartment; and, still, the line for *Priority Gold Star, Black Diamond, Platinum Supernova,* Members was empty; he could skip the line for *all others* and be on his way, though with nowhere to go, the line felt right. In line, he was not special, he was not unique, he was not Colin.

Ages past. Finally, he bought a ticket to Bangkok. It was a flight to somewhere and was far enough away to be his nowhere. It was where he hoped to not find her ghost standing on a corner, walking into a cafe, getting into a cab . . . still entranced.

> *Can't keep hanging on*
> *To all that's death and gone*
> *If you build yourself a myth*[28]

Colin needed to find a part of the world he did not know and would not find memories of her lingering in the faces of others. He wanted to escape and he thought Bangkok far enough.

At the gate Colin was bumped to first class so he found a young traveller, a kid in a faded blue and green knitted hoodie and well-worn flip flops.

"Where's your seat?" he asked the kid.

"Back of the flight, I saved some cash by giving up the leg room I guess," the kid joked. "I didn't even know there was a section below coach."

"Trade?" Colin asked and showed him his ticket.

"What's the deal?"

The kid tried to make eye contact, to read Colin's face, to understand why Colin wanted to give up his seat but could hardly lift his eyes to meet Colin's. Colin scared the kid. It was not his appearance. From a distance Colin looked like most in the City, overworked. His eyes were bloodshot and his hair was disheveled. He wore loafers, demin jeans, a sable collared shirt, and a marengo jacket. It was Colin's intensity that scared the kid. Behind the blood in his eyes was furry

---

[28] "Myth," by Beach House. On *Bloom*. Sub Pop Records and Bella Union Records. March 2012.

and a sadness that suffocated. Standing next to Colin was like being held under water.

"I feel like sitting in shit and your seat'll do. You gonna take the ticket or do I need to ask another broke backpacker trying to get a story from a ping-pong show and a Thai message. Street food, wow! It's been done. Kids need to find a new story."
The kid grabbed the ticket.

"Fuck you. I'm going to teach, but, yeah, I'll take your ticket. You cleared security, right, even if you are a dick."

"Great. Just make sure to find me before you board," Colin warned the kid. He knew TSA would likely take issue with the swap. Plus, it gave him a personal alarm in case he passed out.

The kid grabbed his over-sized, olive-green bag covered in stains and patches from previous travels and walked towards an empty part off the terminal. Colin grabbed his black duffel and walked to the bar. The flight had been delayed.

Here he decided to get drunk. The bar was square. It was built in the middle of the terminal to give travelers quick access in and out. The bartender was female. She was stocky and graceful. She knew every inch of her workspace. She wore a green, polo shirt with the name of the bar stitched in black above her right breast, khakis, and black non-slip shoes.

Can't even choose her own shoes, Colin thought.

She was efficient and knew her clientele. When an overweight man in a blue, button down and black slacks took the open seat to the left of Colin, she quickly made eye-contact.

"Food? Drink?"

Her accent was true to the borough. Her personality true to the City. She was at home in the airport, a place where people were in a hurry and pleasantries were something people with extra time took the time for.

"Both," answered the man and wiped his brow with the white beverage napkin she placed before him.

"Menu?"

"No thanks. Burger mid-well with cheese and a Jack and Diet."

"Fries?"

"Salad with a vinaigrette."

"Got it," she told him and tapped the oval name tag above the pocket on her left breast with her right hand, "Name's Jenny, let me know when you need another," and placed an Old Fashion glass filled with whiskey cola on a fresh bed-nap with her left.

Next she poured a vodka water and garnished the glass with three limes. She placed it in front of Colin and took away the empty glass. She knew not to ask.

Here, Colin had started to forget. He sat and watched his ice melt without thought of the thousands that passed him and the thousands passed without thought of him.

It was easy to forget in an airport. Architects tried to make each unique, to epitomize a city. JFK was designed to welcome visitors and to send them back off with reminders of where they had been. The design was meant to reflect the tastes of the city. But it was blank, stark and drab. It was an empty space used for its necessity. When properly operated a person does not have the time to stroll through the gala of local artists or read the immigrant history of the

City. No one cared to look at the art installation as it hung above or remember the smiling children of the world mural.

Or, maybe they do.

Across the bar he watched passengers as they exited a plane from Heathrow. It was the perfect flight, exactly 8hrs and 15minutes. When Stumblr was launched in London, Colin promoted the app with a 24hr international crawl. The British part ended with breakfast in Farringdon with a lager top, black tea, and a full English and the American part picked back up at lunch with an IPA and a slice at Joe's in the West Village. The flight was long enough a party goer could get an undisturbed six hours of sleep. Naturally, Colin and his team did not sleep. The plane had full bar service and they were on a bar crawl.
Thirty-five thousand feet in the air, the six of them cleaned the plane of vodka and tomato juice.

Colin smiled and forgot about Sarah as he remembered London. Then he forgot about London and remembered Sarah. Near the end of the procession of exiting passengers were four pink faces and unsure steps. It was a hen party on a crawl of their own. Three were in silver dresses and red shoes. The other was in a striped silver and black dress with black shoes. The three matching ladies wore black sashes with military ranks spelled out in gold: *General, Lieutenant,* and *Captain*. The other wore a red sash with *Prisoner* spelled out in silver.

The Lieutenant took the lead and turned the group toward the bar. "Stop in for a bevvy?"

"G'wed round on me, we got time b'fore the bags show," commanded the General.

They ordered four gin and tonics.

"Preference on gin?" Jenny asked.

"Nothin' from London," shouted the Captain.

"Fuckin' right! I won't be drinkin' anythin' from that shite shaty," replied the Prisoner. They all laughed, an inside joke and slight at their London rivals.

The ladies finished their cups in a single go. As they left to collect their bags, Colin heard the Prisoner's phone, Gerry and the Pacemakers.

When you walk through the storm[29] . . .

"You know the rules," barked the General at the Prisoner and the song was quieted.
Colin turned back to his drink.

"8:15 to Bangkok, right?" Jenny interrupted and replaced his drink.

"Yeah."

"Flight's canceled. Help desk is down the terminal. Here's your tab."

"Thanks."

Colin paid the tab and finished the drink. A line had formed at the help desk. It was the standard pissed off, *what happened to my flight,* crowd.

"Oh. I see. You can stop my flight but can't stop terrorism," observed one old wrinkled man to an attendant.

Yeah cause this Delta concierge writes policy for Homeland Security, dumbass, thought Colin.

---

[29] "You'll Never Walk Alone," by Gerry and the Pacemakers. On *Don't Let the Sun Catch You Crying.* Laurie Records and United Artists Records. November 1964. Originally written by Richard Rogers and Oscar Hammerstein II. 1945.

The booze had worked. He was able to forget about Sarah and direct his anger at this *dumbass*. It felt good to be angry, so he listened, commented, and acted towards the pissed off passengers from the confusion and fear of his own loss.

A sense of loss, of being lost, was easy in an airport because an airport was not a destination. It was a place between. How many people came and left was the sole purpose of the place; yet, when an airport lost its purpose and people become stuck in transit, they asked, *Why am I here?* Passengers transposed their purpose, their trip into the sole reason for why an airport exists. They forgot that they are not alone. They feel stranded, isolated and in this confusion, without their purpose, they become fearful. From their fear, they become hostile and angry and enraged asked, *Why am I here?* Then look for someplace, something, someone to place blame with.

That person right there, they screamed in revelation, as they stared at a name tag and company logo.

In an airport it was easy to find blame. One only had to look at the sign posted on every desk, *For faster service, please visit any of our automated kiosks*. These signs told the passengers that even the airlines knew these men and women behind the desk were not essential. The perceived values of the attendants were less than the scales that checked baggage weight or the metal detectors and x-ray machines that scanned passengers and carry-ons. The sole job of the attendant was to ensure the needs of the passengers were met; and, since the passengers' immediate need was to leave and they were not, the attendant was at fault.

"This attendant's mother should have canceled her. I'm surprised she's made it this far," whispered a middle-aged lady to her travel companion. The two snickered.

Cause abortion's a monthly subscription. Cancel any time.

This malice was baseless and the fault was misplaced. It was because a person did not understand the delay. *Don't they know how important this flight is,* a traveler too easily thought, as if only his flight, her trip, that one flight, that one trip was all that mattered.

Most people do not stop to understand a delay. Instead, they related the most intricate of human transportation complexities to the app on their phone that delivered pizzas to their current location with a single click. *I should already be there!* they declared as if the delays were purposefully devised by the attendants to boggle up their plans.

Colin had forgotten Sarah as he mused how insignificant each complaining passenger was. He had done the math before.

Each day 160,000 people passed through the 128 gates at JFK; and a plane left roughly every hundred seconds. Which meant a person is only one passenger is 1 of 1250 passengers an attendant saw at a single gate. A single person is tiny, an unnoticed .08% of the whole mass of travelers for that gate for that day.

Now he simply thought, *you ain't worth dick. You squabbling insignificant . . .*

"Just because you're on the rag doesn't mean you get to . . ." said someone to someone else, somewhere.

Stupid . . .

To travel by flight, people chose to become part of a machine of scheduled wonder. A schedule made by and a machine controlled by other people. It was easy to understand a passenger's fear of being lost in transit, forgotten by these other people in the buzz of *how can there be this many people, doing this many things?* The average person on a plane saw two hundred people they did not know, going and moving in the same direction but for different and unknown reasons. When animals migrated, they migrated as a whole with instinctive purpose. When humans traveled, they scattered like drops of water when a child splashed in a puddle. It was chaos, and the dumb and confused, believed unnoticed, people acted as such.

A black man called a white woman sexist then a white woman called a black man racist. A first-generation Chinese student called a middle-aged Hispanic woman communist.

People worried how often the machine forgot and were they the next to be forgotten? They were dependent on a system they did not understand and were scared. In their anger, they found someone to blame and they lashed out, *You! You are the reason my world has stopped!*

These passengers needed a response to their ignorance, confusion, and fear to understand their situation. They felt the need to gain control and to mask their fears. There was no re-assemblance of self when someone yelled towards a broken plane. They needed a reaction and they found that reaction when they degraded those trying to help. They feel themselves better than, smarter than, the system because they were able to find the fault in it. They alone have found the one part of the machine that is not the perfect piece for that specific task, the *let me point you to a kiosk that does my job more effectively* attendant. They let ignorance govern their confusion. They became scared and did not care or did not think to care of different possibilities.

They would not think that maybe, *just maybe*, their flight was canceled after a plane was rerouted when a passenger had a heart attack or because a part was not repaired on time when the lead engineers went into early labor.

When scared, a person froze and was stuck only to think of the possibility that caused the fear. A scared child cannot assume the noise in the dark the compression of air in the pipes when the scared child first believed the noise a monster. The traveler, in their fright and confusion, cannot assume anything but the imperfect people to be at fault. Then, when the blame was placed upon them, the attendants, those faulty people behind the desks, used the misplaced cliché of the service industry, *the customer is always right*, and apologized for the situations as if a storm in the Pacific or a broken turbine or a sick pilot was of the attendants' making. Before the angry guest was ignorant, confused, and scared. Now their anger was justified, and they walked away from the experience with fresh confidence in the confirmed knowledge that they were right. So, the next time, under the guise of perceived insight based upon a previously conjured reality, they will be even more emboldened.

"I told you, they're completely useless. We're never flying Delta again," commented a man to his travel partner as the two walked from the desk. The man had found the reason to justify his anger, his ignorance, his fear, and his confusion. Delta, a company, a thing that was used for its convenience, was humanized. It became they and they were to blame. The complications of the system were trivialized because they were not understood and, because of his incompetence, the man placed blame to that which he related, that which he believed himself to understand, the *incompetent and replaceable* young man behind the desk.

Colin had long since resigned his commentary to simple, unfocused anger.

Dumb. Stupid. Assholes.

He needed a drink.

Colin walked up to the desk and saw the young man. Mark was tagged and pinned on his uniform. His thick NYC skin was bruised but it kept him safe enough from most insults. He was a professional. When he looked up, he made eye contact and politely asked Colin for his ticket.

"Shit brains," Colin remarked and nodded his head towards the bickering couple that moments before had lashed out.
Mark smiled and quickly moved the conversation.

"Just another day. So, Mr. Lukends, sorry but this ticket does not match your ID."

"Dammit, that's right." Colin had forgotten the trade with the young backpacker. "Give me a second."

Colin found the kid with his ticket. "He needs your ID and my ticket," he told him and led them to the desk as other passengers mumbled complaints and cursed him for the additional delay.

"Okay. Are you to flying together? Because we have a few options," Mark began.

"No. It's just me. He's on his own," Colin told Mark and flicked his head towards the kid to take a step back into line.

"Okay, since it is only you Mr. Lukends, the next flight to Bangkok will not be until tomorrow. Storms have stopped all flight in and out of BKK. We can get you part of the way to L.A. then the rest of the way in the morning. Or . . ."

"Let's skip Bangkok. I'm trying to get out of town immediately and LA is terrible. When and where is the next international flight going."

"Um, okay. Bum. Bum. Bum . . .

She was everywhere.

. . . Shanghai, you would need a visa."

Colin shook his head.

"Tokyo. Paris. Berlin."

She was everywhere.

"No thanks, somewhere remote, someplace no one wants to go to."

"Okay, okay, let me look."

"Alright, I think I found . . ." Mark continued.

By that time, Colin had nearly fallen asleep. Head pressed in his right hand with his elbow propped on the desk, his elbow slid and the jolt shook him awake; startled at first where he was.

". . . San Pedro Sula, Honduras. You'll connect in Atlanta. They're boarding in 15 minutes in the next terminal."

"Perfect."

"However, your checked luggage might not make the flight."

"Don't have any," Colin replied and lifted his duffel.

"Wonderful. Well, here is your ticket Mr Lukends. And, again, we do apologize about the delay and any inconveniences it has caused you. Travel safe and thank you for continuing to fly with Delta."

Colin did not remember boarding the plane or the flight to Atlanta. When he landed, he found the flight to San Pedro Sula was also delayed so he found another bar. Other than a few trivial changes, the bar was identical to the one in New York. SweetWater 420 Pale Ale had replaced Brooklyn Lager and a guy named Brett in a baby blue polo had replaced Jenny in her green.

Still can't choose his own shoes.

Colin stared at the planes of dark wood on the wall across the bar. "I Want You," by the Beatles played in the background.

She's so heavy . . . heavy . . . heavy . . . heavy[30]

---

[30] "I Want You," by the Beatles. On *Abbey Road*. Apple Records. September 1969.

He drank with his back to the terminal and the glass wall where a child stared in wonder at the manmade birds with wings of fiberglass as they left from and came to. The child wore black on white Adidas Originals, jeans tapered with elastic, and a spotted t-shirt. She pressed her face and both hands against the glass. When an engine started, she froze and stood in awe. She watched as the engines warmed and she listened to the air as it was pulled through the turbines and jumped at the hiss when the breaks released. As the plane propelled forward and rose, she ran and followed it along the glass and marveled as the giant gently lifted off the ground and took its place in the sky. She yelled for her mother to look and her breath left the outline of where her puffy cheeks had pressed against the glass, where she had strained to follow the airplane in want of being pull along with it. *Can there really be such a wonderful thing? Just really? Wow!* she gaped, but she did not trust her eyes, she could not believe what she saw and cried for her mother to substantiate the miracle, "Mommy. Mommy. Look. Look!"

"Flight's boarding," Brett told Colin.

He was the last to board and walked to the back. He passed his empty seat in first class, people adjusting neck pillows in priority, and parents unpacking headphones for their children in economy. In the last row, he found a grandmother and traded his seat for hers.

"*I think you might need the extra leg room a bit more than me,*" he told her.

Then he took the seat between a lanky young kid and a tiny old man.

The vodka and the lack of sleep and the emotional exhaustion forced him to sleep before the stewardess walked down the aisles checking seat belts. When he woke, he forgot where he was. Then he remembered when he looked down and saw an aluminum tray, compartmentalized with a breaded fillet of fish, a small salad of iceberg lettuce, radish, a cherry tomato, and two slices of cucumber, a sealed plastic bowl of mandarins in water, *cause fruit doesn't come in its own wrapping,* and a small piece of lemon pound cake in plastic, on top the drop tray folded out of the seat before him. The pound caked had a cartooned face of a girl with big cheeks and pigtails. *It's Delicious!* in yellow bubble letters was written in a word box with pink background. The pound cake had an expiration date seven years off.

He did not think so he ate. A flight attendant asked him if he would like a drink. He ordered a double vodka and cranberry. He finished the drink as he stared past the old man and into the dark night. Then from the other side, Elliot Smith whispered and softly played.

> *Drink up, baby, look at the stars*
> *I'll kiss you again, between the bars*

Finally, he had stopped. The noise had stopped. He was headed someplace else.

So alone, he cried and slept.

> *Where I'm seeing you there, with your hands in the air*
> *Waiting to finally be caught*[31]

---

[31] "Between the Bars" by Elliot Smith. On *Either/Or*. Killer Rock Stars Records. February 1997.

Now

They walk the few blocks to the hostel and, as Rose opens the door to the room, Colin tells her "I've gotta go."

The sun had set, and the tabletop lantern lights the room in that florescent scarlet. The curtains are open and, as the lights from the cars on the street below pass, shadows dance a penumbral ballet. Colin feels watched and listened to. He feels caught and accused or caught and in wait of being waiting accused. He knows what he did, but he has told no one and no one has told him. He can still lie to himself, edit, change, rewrite the truth because he still narrates the story. It is his and, if he wishes, he can keep it buried like so much else. When no one knows his truth, he can hide it.

"Figured. You got that jittery look back at the bar and I knew you wouldn't stay the night."

Rose takes off her jacket. She is glad for this night and is now glad Colin is not going to stay. She had remembered the simple pleasure off being around those who loved her. That bar, that place, the familiar smell of wax and whiskey, the chairs worn from years of use—people had cried, laughed, loved, fought in, with, and over those seats—it was her home. It still is. It is the place she last saw her father.

"Off course," Pete's quick answer when Rose had asked him to host her father's wake. "And don't you insult me and try to pay. I'll be glad to have one last drink with your Paps."

Nearly in tears, Rose thinks of how much love is between those walls and she does not know why it had taken a drunk, broken and wondering, to lead her back there.

Unlike Colin, she is in search of her past and this night reminds her of how much of it she still has. For so long, too long, she has been with Colin. At some point, he took point. He led her along his path and it is not a path she would have chosen alone. It is from circumstance that she follows and it is a kindness that he leads but it is euthanasia. She forgot that her definition of self is through those she serves and, in the past months, she has only served herself, a pitiful, lonesome version of it.

"No. I have to go," he repeats. She looks at him and sees he is terrified. He too is almost in tears. "I'm sorry . . ."

Rose turns to Colin. He stands in the doorway, unable to enter, hesitant to move. He is shaking and terrified.

"What happened?" she asks then checks her own panic. "Where will you go?"

She knew one day he would leave. She did not think it would be today.

Why today?

She almost asks him to stay but knows she cannot. She needs him to go. And, how could she ever ask him to stay, when she had always known his truth.

BEFORE

ROSE

"Where will you go?" Rose asked Colin when he was cleared from the hospital in Honduras.

It was a month after the interview with the cops and he had recovered enough that the doctors judged him safe to travel.
A week before, 150,000 American was transferred to the hospital. It was part of Sarah's life insurance. Always the planner, she had the policy since she was 18 and it totaled half a million. Colin had asked for the entire sum to be transferred. His attorney, Stumblr's attorney, had called the hospital without his knowledge and asked for Colin's bill, post insurance.

Over the past month, Colin had talked little, still Rose knew he would not go home. The media had picked up on his story and she had read the headlines: *Young start-up CEO found beaten in Honduras after missing wife's funeral, Heartbroken Wiz Kid found body broken in Central America, Missing Developer found in third world hospital, NYC'r survives Murder Capital of the World!*

She knew who Sarah was and knew how she died. Very little else about the story interested her, Colin was in front of her and needed her help and, true to self, she gave it to him.

"I don't know. Figure I'll start the same way I did before, there's a bar in the airport, right?"

He smiled but it faded. His eyes were clear, for the past week he had been on mild sedatives, mostly Ibuprofen. However, he had become haunted. Before it was only Sarah. Now there was Katryna as well.

In Sarah's death, he felt he had lost his life. His life, he felt, had cost Katryna hers.

"It's not your fault," she told him.

"If I had not gotten on an airplane to Honduras, would she still be alive?" he asked her.

She had no answer.

"Tell me!" he ordered though to Rose it sounded like a plea.

"I don't care about what they did to me," he told her. "I care about what they did to her because of me. I found that bar. I fucking searched for that bar. You think another person would have been such a fool? I walked into that bar because I wanted a way out, a way to leave my life behind, and instead I got a girl killed because she thought I was a way out, a way for her to leave her life behind. She expected me to have clout. Everyone must have thought me of some importance since I wasn't knifed on the spot, but I was not important. I'm not important. Instead, I was a stupid, pathetic, drugged out drunk. I was selfish and lonely and I got her killed."

This was the most Colin had spoken to Rose about the night he was hospitalized. She did not have the answers he needed but he needed help, something she did have, so she asked again, "So where next? Where are you going?"

"Somewhere I can be pathetic, lonely and stupid without getting someone killed. I don't know. Not home, I don't even know where that would be."

"Here, take this."

She handed him a business card. It was black with *Slainte* embossed in velvet letters. "It's my favorite bar in Dublin. I get drinks there every Tuesday night I'm home and this will get you a free drink."

"Thanks but . . . "

"It's a drink ticket to a bar in a town with a bunch of sad, lonely drunks," she smiled. "And if you're lucky, I might have a place for you to stay for a while. You know, somewhere to figure yourself out."

He took the card. Then he grabbed his bag, a black duffel, and told her thanks. Colin left and she went back to work.
Rose returned to Dublin after her leave of absence.

The second week back, Colin was at Slainte. It was a sleek, modern bar on North Quay. She was surprised to see him but glad he had come. He was clean shaven and his eyes were clear with only a thin gloss, like ice that has yet to freeze moving water. They chatted and she took him home.

He stayed until he remembered.

Now

"Where will you go?" she repeats.

He takes a breath and tries to calm himself. He looks at Rose and, for that second, he sees only Rose. He hugs her and kisses her.

"Thank you," he tells her. "Now, please forget about me, I will never be who you want and I never was who you needed."

Then he sees Sarah as a sheet is pulled over her, he sees Katryna as she is dragged away, and he sees Dickie as blood pools under his head.

"I'm sorry. I gotta go."

Outside he bums another cigarette then walks down Deverell Place, a small side road across from of the hostel. He knows to stay off the main beats and to avoid any known faces. The road ends and he winds his way through the back alleys between buildings. Soon the alley ends and opens into a small square. Above and behind him is a clocktower, its white face a mirror of the moon, and atop it is a small, oxidized copper dome. Directly ahead, to the west of the clocktower, rests a giant's hand cast in bronze. Cut at the wrist, the hand sits palm up as if to ask those who pass, *How may I help?* On a plaque next to the hand is written, *The Wishing Hand by Linda Brunker.* Beyond the statue is Malborough Street and across it a chapel, the Liffey Street Mass House men called it before.

Now atop the chapel sits St. Mary's Pro Cathedral, the seat of the Catholic Church in Ireland. The building is stoic, simple, and plain. It is square and crowned with a cupola coated in patina. The doors of the church open to the east and behind stone Doric pillars that dominate the façade and hold up the pediment. Three stone carved saints stand watch on each corner of the gable. It is built to remind one of antiquity as if the pillars uphold some sense of the neoclassical philosophy of justice. The church is cold, unwelcoming. From outside it seems a place one goes to be judged when summoned, not a place one seeks to find forgiveness.

Colin walks along the black iron fencing. A nomad, a vagabond, leans against the oversized stone foundation and strums a small guitar. His hair is shaggy, his clothes loose and light. Beside him sits a case open to collect the money he trades for his songs.

> *Thought I heard some woman screaming*
> *And I sat up in my bed*
> *And I went over to the window*
> *I saw him in the cold street, lying dead*
> *Oh, please tell me, you academics*
> *How do you wake up from a non-dream . . .*

Colin steps through a gate and walks up the narrow stone steps. He enters the church because it is open and he doubts any disciple knows him. He does not want to find God. The last time he was in a church was for his grandmother's funeral. The last time he prayed was the night in the hospital when he remembered Katryna. Since, he had given up on prayers. They had failed him. Still, he needs sanctuary.

Inside, the church opens. It is colossal. It is classic and ornamental. To the left of Colin is a simple prayer altar to Mary, the Mother of Jesus. To the right is a prayer altar of Jesus on the Cross. Small candles are lit before the altars. Each candle is a prayer offered and a call to intercession. Further in more prayer alters with icons and relics line the side walls. In front of Colin the room is split by a central aisle, each side with twenty rows of pews. On the floor of the aisle a mosaic of colorful tiles, gold, silver, blue, and green, circles to the front altar. To the side of the dark oak pews are more stone pillars that support the heavy and arched ceiling above. The central cupola gives depth and space to what appears flat and shallow outside. The cupola is lined with four rows of dark, square framed windows. The windows circle and compress with the curve of the dome. Under the cupola are four arches and the Ascension of Jesus is carved into the stone of the western most arch. The main altar is set at the far end of the room. The top is marble. The base is stone, light and polished, and on the front of the stone base, two angels are carved and set forever on their knees in adoration of their Lord. Behind the alter Mary, stained in glass, stands watch over the earth. Even at night, the colors are vibrant. Green, red, yellow, and blue highlight the white stone alter. To Mary's left is St. Laurence O'Toole, the father of Irish Catholics.

God knows, I have not a penny under the sun to leave anyone.

His grandmother used to say that every time Colin asked her for money. He does not know why he thought of this.

Why now?

To Mary's right is St. Kevin with his blackbird.

> *Imagine being Kevin, Which is he?*
> *Self-forgetful or in agony all the time . . .*

There is a small crowd gathered in prayer near the front alter. An old woman sits in the front row. Her quiet sobs occasionally echo in the cavernous space and, in those small moments, the walls seem in pain. Behind her several Garda Siocana stand at attention. They seem as statues themselves the Garda, the guardians, in their dress blues with peak caps tucked under their right arms.

Colin walks to the left away from the guards.

He passes several more alters where candles are lit and prayers have been offered. He takes a seat in the pew before a Celtic Cross. The Cross is ten feet tall. It is worn bronze and is in contrast to the polished gold, silver, copper, and brass of the surrounding icons, the glossed stone columns and marble statues, and the varnished wood. This cross is dark. It is Gothic. It screams pain. Along its base, a man in cast on his knees before Mary and in veneration of the Cross. A chain wraps along the statue and binds the man to Mary and to the Cross. At the foot of the cross and before the man are four bottles. It is here the chain is broken. The statue, the cross, the man, the chain, is haunting.

Colin does not want mercy. He believes himself beyond forgiveness. Still, he sits and, in obligation, tries to pray. He looks at his hands. They are shaking. He pulls his flask from his jacket. It is still empty. He looks at the empty, tarnished bronze bottles at the foot of the Cross, and he looks at the face of the man in veneration, fearful, humble, and ashamed.

BEFORE

COLIN

"Blanco, I am sorry what happened to your friend," spoke a soft voice. He thought it a ghost.

"I'm sorry, blanco," the voice repeated. The accent was thick but gentle.

Colin sat up and scanned the room and found the old man across the room in Bed 6 awake.

"What do you mean? What friend?" Colin asked.

"Katryna. The one spoken to the doctor about."

"What do you know about her?"

"I tell you this story more for me. I haven't told it in full before and it might help us both to listen to it," explained the man.

After his interview with the cops, Colin was taken back to the ICU and then, after the doctors, nurses, and cops left and the hospital became quiet and its residents slept, the old man with the worn features spoke again.

"I'm sorry about your friend," the man began and coughed and blood spotted the inner elbow of his Johnny gown. "My name is Pedro. I would like to tell you my story."

Colin remained silent.

"There are many things in my country that speak truth, our religion, our identity, who we believe ourselves to be; however, my country is not Honduras. Honduras is corruption. You found that. Walk down the streets of the cities and you do not find humanity, you find frustration, fear, anger, and hate. We speak of countries that were not created by the people who fill them. People are communities. Honduras is not people. Honduras is not a community. Honduras is bananas. Honduras is the man outside defining the land inside by its value to him.

I am sorry. I am talking too far from my story.

Let me start, where I did. I was born in Chiligatora, a small village a day south of the Pulhapanzak Falls. A place few tourists go. We have a larger waterfall than at Pulhapanzak, the Rio Grande, but it is not easy to get to. My family is one of the last natives to this land. When I was young many Americans and other white Europeans traveled to our hills to help us. I became close with one. His name was Robert Wilson. Bobbie, we called him. He believed the world to be a community and he is how I speak your language.

Bobbie came from Washington, the capital of your place. Born to a family of artists, his father was a painter and his mother made success selling the works of others. She sold many works but few paintings by the father of Bobbie. From her life, they lived well, and Bobbie was able to travel. First, he followed after his brother then he went further. The youngest of his family, he felt he needed to prove himself. What I know of his younger years are only a few, small stories, when we would sit down and talk free.

I found that he was the man I knew because of a belt. 'You always wear a belt,' Bobbie would often say. One day, I told him I did not own one and asked what was the importance of a belt. First, he gave me the one he wore. I remember we had to make several new holes because it was too big. Then, with a smile, he repeated, 'You always wear a belt,' and told me that when he was 13, he went to meet a girl and his older brother told him to put on a belt. 'You always wear a belt,' his brother shouted as he ran out the door. To Bobbie this was a lesson of, what is the word, expectations?"

Colin nodded and made a soft sound in agreement.

"The lesson of the belt taught him that the world has expectations of you that you are unaware of. You must always be willing to learn, to change, to 'put on a belt.' To Bobbie this meant he too must teach others what is expected. When I asked him the truth in the lesson of the belt, he told me, 'You never want to get caught with your pants down, 'specially in front of a pretty woman.'

Pedro chucked.

"He lived several summers with us in our homes in the hills without lights or water. Then he moved here, to San Pedro Sula, to start a school. He asked me to leave my village and work with him. He wanted to teach the kids of Honduras that they deserved more than what they had been given. They did not have to steal, lie and kill their way through life. They only had to find a passion and follow it. He loved the work, but the kids did not respect him. They did not respect me. The streets taught them not to trust so they did not.

The school he started, that I helped, was not from nothing. To start, money came from donations from the patrons of the galleries of his mother. Twice a year, he and I visited the United States when his mother hosted auctions to raise money for the school. But then donations stopped. There was a coup in Honduras and the American patrons stopped their donations. They were worried about the instability of the country and that their money could not be used properly. Or, that is what they claimed. Bobbie tried to explain that only education would bring change, but his words were not heard, their ears were closed. So, he become desperate.

In La Esperanza, a community just next to Chiligatora, Bobbie was made known to the drug smugglers in the area. La Esperanza was off the grid, a peaceful mountain area that no one took the time to look into. The region was farmland, poor and undeveloped. The smugglers took advantage and paid the community to look the other way. That is, they paid those in the community who had enough power to be of concern to them. Anyone who spoke up was quieted. Drugs harm more people as it is moved than they will ever harm the users.

During his first summers in Honduras, Bobbie supplied the village with cement, timber, brick, solar . . . anything he could to help my family and friends. In order to work without questions and to travel safely in the area, Señor Fonseca, a leader in the area and the point of contact to the smugglers, took his share of the supplies. Bobbie despised the man but did not open his mouth. Señor Fonseca had purpose and some power, much less that he imagined but he had enough; and, Bobbie knew he might need the help of Señor Fonseca so he did not aggravate this relationship with his opinions.

When funding from America stopped, Bobbie forsook his ethics and asked Señor Fonseca for help. Señor Fonseca introduced Bobbie to a man named Marco. Marco was known, he was a powerful man, and through Marco Honduras opened to Bobbie. Marco understood that money could be sent through a business with the right stretch and the school needed money. That year, Bobbie opened the first privately funded charter school for the poor youth in San Pedro Sula with drug money. Marco even introduced Bobbie to the Mayor and then the President.

That first year two hundred kids were selected to attend. It was hard telling kids of the street once again they were not wanted but we had only so much space. One child came in wearing only cut off shorts, no shirt, and no shoes. We asked him how old he was, he did not know. We gave him a puzzle, a 3D cut out of Notre Dame. He spent the day looking at the pieces and the picture of a building he had never seen. He finished the puzzle then left after, we could only guess, he thought he was again forgotten. Bobbie spent two weeks looking for the kid. He wanted him to attend but the child was never found.

A few years after the school graduated its first class, a young man asked to see Bobbie. By then the school had grown to over five hundred students and he claimed to be a brother of one of the students. I walked in as the boy ran from the office. Bobbie was stabbed in the chest, a picture of Notre Dame pinned between the knife and his heart.

I left the school that day and went hunting for the kid. I fell into the streets that Bobbie and I worked to pull kids out of. I became an addict. Before, how I viewed the world with Bobbie, I do not remember. I saved what he taught me in my heart and that has long left. What the streets taught me, I will never forget. Now I understand the look of detest and insecurity in the eyes of the students.

A week ago, I found him, the kid who killed Bobbie. I found the kid with six others like him. All pathetic and all useless. Their purpose to kill and destroy the purpose of others because they never found theirs. I asked him if he knew Notre Dame. He smirked, nodded, and tapped the chest of one of his friends. The rest laughed."

Colin had grown impatient, tired of the story. He only needed one thing from this man, this murderer.

"How did you know Katryna?" asked Colin.

"I did not. But the kid who killed Bobbie was named Henry, Henry Verela. I strangled him with the belt Bobbie gave me."

Pedro pulled the blanket off his body and lifted his right hand. It was handcuffed to the bed.

"Me he vengado si eres el tipo hombre que lo necesita."

Now

Colin stands. His story finished. He takes out the money he stole from a dead man, the man, Richard, Dickie, he had killed then robbed and left in the street. Most of the money he had spent or given to Rose. There is maybe eighty euros. He pockets a twenty note and shoves the rest into the donation box next to the dark Cross and gold plaque. *The Veneration of Matt Talbot by Timothy Schmalz* is inscribed on the plaque. Colin lights a candle, again, in obligation.

> *. . . A prayer his body makes entirely*
> *For he has forgotten self, forgotten bird*
> *And on the riverbank forgotten the river's name*
> *-Seamus Heaney*

He grabs his duffle and starts to leave. He walks past the columns and the pews and the altars from before. At the altar of Jesus on the Cross, now stands the old women and her guardians. She is in grief, but she bears it. When she looks at the altar, her lips press together and her eyelids flutter. She lightly rocks back and forth as she looks into the face of a man crucified. She touches the man's feet and apologizes as only a mother can.

Colin slows his walk. He does not want to pass in front of the officers, but his slowed pace draws the attention of the woman. She does not move to leave, as Colin had hoped, but instead invites him to her with a gesture of her hand.

He obeys.

"Did you know my son?" she asks after she has taken his hand in hers.

"Your son?"

"Richard. Richard Donnogaul. This vigil is for him."

She had lost her son.

"Richard?"

"Yes. Did you know him?"

He does not answer. He did not know. He does not know. He lets go of her hand. This is what he saw in her eyes, the grief of a mother who has lost her son, and this grief, this grief she bore, he knew he was the cause of. He had killed Richard. He had killed her son. Before Colin felt his life lost when Sarah passed and he knew his life had cost Katryna hers. But now he had killed. Now he had taken a life from others.

"I'm . . . I . . ." he tries to respond, nothing. How can he answer this question? He cannot.

Tears begin. He tucks his heads into his right shoulder, covers his face with his left hand, and hides his tears out of fear. He knows the tears are true but he is scared she will recognize the truth, his truth and he will be made known. So, he hides in the tears, excuses himself, and turns to leave. At the doors, he tumbles and falls down the steps.

The traveller stares and sings:

> . . .*No, it ain't no dream, it's all too real*

Drunk, stupid, and afraid, he runs. Where to, he does not know. He cannot think. His feet lead: north on Marlborough, second right, through the alleys and straight to Railway, straight through to Killarney Ave then against traffic on Killarney Street. He slows and coughs. His is winded but forces himself to walk, to stagger against the headlights and follow North Stand. He crosses over the Tolka River, the northernmost of Dublin's rivers, and walks into Fairview Park, a small park along the eastern coastline.

The sounds of the city fade. The feel of the city fades. The park is quiet and Colin is alone. He needs, he wants, again he confuses the two, to leave. At the far side of the park he finds help. He spends the twenty on beer and buys a few loosies with the change. Outside he finishes two beers, tosses the cans in the bin next to the shop, and opens a third. He walks into the park and, somewhere around the eighth beer, he disappears.

> *How long until*
> *This river of blood congeals?*
>
> *Bum bum bum*[32]

---

[32] "Bum Bum Bum," by Cass McCombs. On *Mangy Love*. Anti- Records. August 2016.

BEFORE

COLIN

Bum...bum...bum... Colin woke up as men and women clapped to the sound of the airplane as it bounced on the tarmac and the kid to his right stared out the window. There was no skyline and there were no stars. Clouds covered and blacked out the sky. As the plane approached the terminal, a faint light slowly overtook the dark. It was the trivial, single terminal airport. Quietly, the plane docked and, slowly, the guests exited. The airport was silent, the flight was late. Security was minimal. A lone customs agent checked in the travelers. No one cared who came into Honduras and the agent could no longer fake his concern. It was the end of his shift, he wanted to go home, and without a glance at Colin or his passport, he stapled the customs slip, and silently ushered Colin into Honduras with a wave of his hand.

Besides the cleaners, the terminal was still. Near the exit, a small donut shop remained open. Colin's head stung. He wished he had bought a mini from the flight attendant before he stepped off the plane. He needed something and figured a coffee would help keep him focused on that need.

A young man in a white polo and brown slacks was cleaning the shelves behind the counter.

"Lo siento, la comida se fue," the man told him and hoped his Spanish would ward off the American.

"Café?"

"Si."

He ordered the coffee and paid with an American twenty.

"Lo siento. Necesito conseguir algo . . . ¿Cuál es tu moneda?" Colin asked the young man behind the counter.

"Lempira, Señor," the man replied.

"Guarde el cambio, cámbielo mañana."

"Gracias."

Colin sipped the coffee, "¿Buen café, local?

"Es de Etiopía, buenas noches Señor," the kid told him and turned to clean the shelves.

Two booths from the sugar and cream, in the far corner of the room, away from the terminal, a couple sat at a brown table in an orange, fan back booth and talked to a cop. Both were neither small nor large. The woman wore sunglasses that bugged her eyes and a white blouse with colorful hibiscuses printed on it. The man wore a white t-shirt with a dive flag, red with a white diagonal stripe, above the right breast pocket and sunglasses that hung on a string around his neck. At home, they would have been considered tan, but they were not home, as the day reminded them.

"You were waiting for the hotel van to pick you up after your flight had been canceled?" asked the cop.
He was a beat officer in a dark blue uniform and black bulletproof vest with *Policia* in white stenciled between the shoulder blades. He held a small notebook and, as Colin added cream to his coffee, he read back his notes to the couple. They were both shaken. The woman did not talk. When the man did, his voice was nervous, and his words were quick and airy.

"Yes sir."

"You were sitting here, and your wife was across from you," repeated the cop and motioned to his seat then that of the man.

"That's right."

"Then a man in a very large black t-shirt, black New York Yankees hat, and large sunglasses sat next to your wife."

The man nodded.

"The man who sat down then said he had a gun. He said it was pointed at your wife then asked you to hand over your bag; the bag you had only moments before packed a camera and tablet into. Then you leaned and placed the bag on the floor next to him. It was then that you saw the gun. At this point, he threatened to kill her if you . . . ."

Colin did not hear nor care about the story. He exited the shop with his twenty-dollar coffee and looked around for a place to get some cash.

He found an ATM and withdrew the maximum. Then shoved the sixty thousand into the side pocket of his bag, he had no idea if this was a little or a lot of money. He just hoped it was enough for a room and a drink. He had slowly become sober and sober was not good. Sober, he was lucid and he could regret this decision. In his desperation to escape, he had become trapped within the consequences. He wanted to leave, so he left. That decision led him to be alone in a part of the world that he did not know or understand. He knew nothing of San Pedro Sula and, even if he asked for direction, he did not know where they would lead.

Outside the terminal, it was hot and dry. Immediately, he began to sweat. At the first rubbish bin, he tossed his coffee and accepted that he had again made the wrong decision. Down from the exit was parked a white, four door compact car with numbers boxed in black on the rear passenger doors. The driver waved him inside. It was clean, other than the front, center ashtray, and a burnt fog creep from the crack left in the driver side windows.

"Alcohol y algún lugar barato para quedarse. No hay turistas," Colin told the driver.

The car drove towards the high-rise lights of the city center in the distance. From the speakers, Marshall Mathers spoke broken and tormented:

> *In my moments of weakness*
> *I openly admit the shit I wouldn't normally*
> *I'm extremely self-conscious and enormously*
> *Insecure*

"American?" the driver asked over the noise.

"Yeah."

"Fantastic. Americans they got the best stuff. This car is American, 12 years old, bought it used and drove it down from California. This song, American! Eminem, the best! You care?" The driver held up a cigarette.

"No." Then Colin asked for one. He had quit. He had quit for Sarah.

"You know these things will kill you right?" the driver asked and faked a few coughs as he passed back a smoke and a lighter.

Colin lit the cigarette as the driver continued to banter.

"First time in San Pedro Sula?"

"Yeah."

"Spanish good?"

"Si mi abuela me enseño."

"Bien, bien, quieres tener cuidado aquí. Este lugar es peligroso. . ."
Colin pulled at the cigarette and did not listen. His head ached and he regretted tossing the coffee, another stupid decision. Occasionally, he shook his head or made a sound when he felt the driver fell quiet and Colin felt him waiting for a reply. He knew little of Honduras. *Don't go* was the consensus. It had a murder rate higher than New York City did at the height of the crack game in the early ninetys. *Or something like that* he thought as he stared out the window and watched the unknown names on the road signs tick by.

Skylar Grey's voice, soft and sad, broke his thoughts.

> *And all you do is strangle me*
> *Such a beautiful relief*[33]

Earlier than he expected, still far from the city lights, they turned off CA-13, the highway used to travel between the airport and inner city. The neighbor was poor but clean. Little pastel colored houses and shops lined the roads. It could have been quaint, yet, in contrast to the soft colors, dark red and brown steel barred every window and Colin knew every entrance gate was locked from within. The main road was cracked and the side streets were unpaved, dry dirt. The cabbie drove quickly and knowingly. He avoided pots holes and the unlit alleys. Eventually, he stopped at a baby blue, two story building. The ground floor, that looked to be a shop, was dark and apparently closed. Above, on the second floor, there was a small balcony and lights from a TV flashed through the curtains behind the glass of the sliding door. An eight-foot cement battlement painted lavender with pink pillars circled the house.

"Tequila or whiskey?"

---

[33] "Tragic Endings," by Eminem ft Skylar Grey. On *Revival*. Aftermath Records, Interscope Records, and Scope Records. December 2017.

"Tequila."

"Cigarettes?"

"Yeah."

"Seiscientos, quédate aquí."

Colin handed him the cash and the driver exited the car.

At the steel gate painted white, the driver looked up and down the street, unlocked the padlock that hung at the gate, opened the gate, stepped with the walls, relocked the gate, and disappeared into the dark. After a few moments a light in a back room was turned on and Colin saw shadows, cast from the new inner light, move along the far curtain wall. Quickly, the light went off and the driver came back with the bottle and cigarettes in hand.

"Salud," he said and tossed the stash back to Colin.

Colin opened the bottle and drank. He closed his eyes and tried to forget why he was there.

A few blocks from the twenty-four-hour booze and smoke shop, the taxi stopped at a guesthouse in Felipe Zelaya. The house was similar in shape and design to the store. It had two stories and a front facing balcony enclosed by a cement wall and steel gate. Outside, an older woman, greeted Colin. She explained she owned the building and lived on the ground floor and that, if Colin wanted, the upstairs was used as a guesthouse.

Colin thanked her, paid for a week in advance, and walked upstairs.

He had found his nowhere.

NOW

"Hey Rose, it's Colin," shouts Schmitt.

Rose stops wiping down the bar. Her hair is short and bobbed with bangs. She is wearing a black V-neck t-shirt and jeans, the left knee is patched over in black cloth, the patch has *PEACE* stitched in rainbow as a rainbow. She is a few pounds heavier in spirit and body. Her eyes are bright, unburdened of much of her past. She is content and able to process both joy and loss.

She turns to the TV in the corner of the bar. On the screen is a photo of Colin and a headline scrolls, *Breaking News: Colin Lukends Found*. She grabs the remote next to the register and turns up the volume. A tall, handsome blonde anchor, in a dark suit and striped tie, reads the story. His voice is monotone, the key facts of the story are emphasized by the length of the pause between words.

"For months, people have speculated whether Colin Lukends survived his dip in the Black Pool, after he jumped into the River Liffey at the Tom Clarke Bridge.

The founder of Stumblr, an online app that guides users through the nightlife of cities around the world, Mr. Lukends resigned from the company, after his wife died of a brain tumor, a week after they married, and had since seemingly disappeared.

Now it is confirmed that Mr. Lukends did end his own life when Police went to question him out about the murder of Richard Donnogaul, a retired Police Officer from here in Dublin."

The camera cuts from the anchor and flashes to a picture of Colin in a dark blue suit and solid black tie. He is clean shaven and without the deep lines under his eyes. The Stumblr logo is stamped on the bottom right of the frame. Slowly, Colin's photo fades and on screen appears a picture of Mr. Donnogaul in his dress blues. It shows a vibrant, middle aged man. His cheeks are tight and his eyes are clear and wide. Both pictures are a kindness taken years before.

"Mr. Donnogaul was last seen with an American outside a bar in Trinity. Early the next morning, Mr. Donnogaul's body was found in an alley near his home in Smithfield. Quickly, the police identified the suspect as Mr. Lukends."

Next on screen is an aerial view of the River Liffey. Pinned on the image are the Tom Clark Bridge and Smithfield Alley as the camera cuts back to the anchor.

"The body of Colin Lukends has still yet to be found. Leaving room for some to speculate that the well-versed traveler survived his dip into the Black Pool and is in hiding here in Ireland or elsewhere.

Legally, however, Mr. Lukends is presumed dead which leaves the question of who is to inherit his shares in Stumblr, which are estimated to be worth several millions. Still, as is nearly everything with this bizarre story, nothing is clear and, only mere minutes before jumping from Clarke Bridge, Mr. Lukends changed his will to a vague letter. One we assume only the recipient can make sense of.

On the day of his suicide, Mr. Lukends visited Ms. Ryner, an associate at Cain, Mrytle, Screib and Wellers, and amended his will."

A picture of illegible text on papyrus fades and the camera cuts and pans to the front of the office building where Ms. Ryner works. It is an old stone building with dark red doors and deep-set diamond pained windows framed in rusted iron. Ms. Ryner stands in front of the doors. A gold plaque with the name of the law firm is seen to her right. She is short, stern, and attractive in an ash suit top and a dark blue blouse. She wears a small necklace with a gold pedate leaf ornament, and her dark hair is pulled back and up. Her eyes are oak brown.

She begins:

"It was right at 9 am. I had walked to the lobby to check in with Matthew, my assistant, when Mr. Lukends walked in. Mathew asked him how he could be of service. Mr. Lukends informed him he wanted to change his will. He appeared rushed, almost frantic, and somewhat disheveled. The secretary told him that, since he was not a client of the law firm, he would have to schedule an appointment. Mr. Lukends then told Matthew it was an emergency and that he would pay to expedite the service. Again, the secretary told him he was sorry but there was nothing he could do other than schedule an appointment. That's when Mr. Lukends offered an incredibly large amount for someone to change his will in the next fifteen minutes. I have to admit, I was curious, it was a lot of money for such a routine service, so I stepped in and introduced myself.

He paid upfront via a credit card. After, we went into my office and begun the paperwork. Before we finished, or, before I thought we were finished, a siren was heard outside. Immediately, he signed the paperwork, and said, 'I gotta go.'
Two days later, I received a call from Mr. Lukends' attorney in the United States. He wanted to know about the transaction.

Apparently, he had been looking for Colin and this was the first credit card transaction in years."

BEFORE

ROSE

"How well would you say you knew Mr. Lukends?" they asked.

"As well as anyone could. We met in Honduras, then continued our relationship here," Rose answered.

She reached out to the Police after hearing the story. She knew it was Colin. *How could I have been so blind, the blood* and pictured the sleeve of his jacket. At first, she blamed herself. She thought somehow, she was to blame for his decision.

Since he had been interviewed a dozen times, cops, journalists,

"Can you tell me about the relationship?"

"We found ourselves in need of each other, well, I thought we needed each other. It was circumstance. We were both orphans of a kind. We met when we were both in need of support, of help."

After a while, the questions became familiar. They became transitive. Though the repetition of their questions, what was personal, terrifying, *Colin had murdered someone*, had become a point of reflection. The edges to the story, *the red blood, the glances back, the sudden, final goodbye,* were muted, dulled.

Before, she did not believe the story. Then she came to accept it. Now she understood it.

I Hate You. I Love You

She removed herself from it. She learned to love him through the past and not the present. She did not deny that she loved him, a version of him. But came to understand that version was never Colin. She wanted so much to believe that he was somehow sent to her, to save her somehow.

How did you never notice,
You were slowly killing me

Before he had taken her so far away from self. After, when she was without him, she was able to look back and find a version of that self. He had led her, the voice of the prodigal. Without him, her voice had led her home.

Today, she sat in an office, in oversized leather chairs, in front of a dark wood desk, and listened as Ms. Ryner read Colin's Last Will and Testament:

Rose,

Time to stitch up someone else. I did love you as I could. I know that when I looked at you, I too often was looking for someone else. I had hoped, I might see her. Guess it's too late for that.

Whatever I have left is yours. I don't know what that means, I don't know what's left. I guess I haven't known for a while.

Don't let them put Roses on my grave, they'll never compare. Lillies, perhaps.

Forget about me and remember who you are. Back to work.

-Colin

Rose had known not to hope for an apology. Colin did not want forgiveness. He had created his hell.

And, only after she had stepped away from his fire, did she see his delusion and hers.

You want her, you need her
And I'll never be her[34]

She had hoped the moments of love he showed her would amplify. It was not until after, that she realized those moments were his last.

Forget about me and remember who you are, she heard the words.

Colin ensured his pain would be eternal. She let him go in order to live with hers.

---

[34] "I Hate U, I Love U," by Gnash ft. Olivia O'Brien. On *We*. Atlantic Records. February 2016.

Now

The camera cuts from outside the law firm and the viewers are returned to the newsroom as the anchor continues to narrate.

"Before, this credit card transaction ultimately led police to conclude, it was Colin Lukends that they saw jump into the River Liffey from the Tom Clarke Bridge. Now it is certain."

Rose turns off the TV and watches Sam and Schmitt pick up their glasses, toss back the remains, and slide the empties towards her. *Back to work* she thinks and smiles. The smile is sad and torn and happy and forgiving. She remembers the pain of his loss, the pain in having her love, the love that she gave, taken. She is sad she forgot. She remembers the joy of giving that love and having it accepted, when it could be. She forgives him and herself and is both happy and sad. She picks up the empties, refills them and places them on top the beer-soaked coasters in front of the two men. Then she grabs four shot glasses and fills the glasses with Yellow Label.

They lift their glasses and out of the jukebox Billy Corgan, brittle and hoarse, gives the toast, isolated and taut.

> *Obscured*
> *Through these eyes*
> *I rely on all I've seen*
>
> *Obscured*
> *Through these eyes*
> *It looks like I'm home tonight*[35]

"Cheers."

---

[35] "Obscured," by the Smashing Pumpkins. On *Pisces Iscariot*. Virgin Records. October 1994.

Slainte

ABOUT THE AUTHOR

Lance Nation is a Virginia native. Born in Fairfax, he attended highschool in Hampton Roads, college in Harrisonburg, and now residents in Richmond with his wife and their dog.

Although he claims Virginia as his home, he has lived and travelled throughout the United States and abroad. He is professional scuba diver and the founder of the international humanitarian organization Smol Haos Toilet Project.

It's On Repeat is his first novel.

Made in the USA
Middletown, DE
24 September 2022